The Seven Ways of Ayurveda

———

"In *The Seven Ways of Ayurveda*, Sarah demystifies the doshas in a way that empowers you to self-reflect and see your innate qualities on a whole new level. This book arms you with the knowledge to tap into ancient Ayurvedic wisdom to see tangible improvements in your daily life, understand yourself on a deeper plane, and have a whole new perspective on how to bring yourself back into balance for your unique makeup."

—CASSANDRA BODZAK, author of *Eat with Intention* and *Manifesting Through Meditation*

"In this beautiful book, Sarah puts her arms around a vast and ancient science and offers it to us like a sweeping bouquet of nature's delight. Because Ayurveda is a healing science, the doshas have been most fully covered in terms of identifying imbalance and what to do to restore. Sarah turns this around and looks at the doshas in their positive expression, seeing how each does at work, in life, and in love, making this a practical guide for bringing out the best in you. An easy, delightful read, it can open your world in unexpectedly radiant ways."

—LAURA PLUMB, Ayurveda practitioner and teacher, author of *Ayurveda Cooking For Beginners*

"Sarah brings a fun and delightfully playful approach to Ayurveda! This book will empower you with practical knowledge of the doshas in work, in love, and everyday life, so you can confidently care for yourself and uncover your strengths along the way. If you're looking for a renewed relationship with your well-being, one that inspires you to know yourself and live authentically to your true nature, I highly recommend this book."

—CLAIRE RAGOZZINO (VATA-PITTA), author of *Living Ayurveda*

"Dr. Kucera's exceptional talent for clarity and relevance shine in this practical guide to your dosha, or blueprint for achieving optimal health. I've read my fair share of Ayurveda books and this one stands out because Sarah keeps a foot in beginner's soil—she adeptly breaks down complex concepts to feel approachable and actionable to everyone. This book makes you feel deeply seen and understood, then gives you the guidance to not simply survive but thrive as your best self."

—GINA CAPUTO (PITTA-KAPHA), E-RYT 500, health and wellness coach and founder of the Colorado School of Yoga

"Expanding the concept of 'dosha' beyond food lists and body types, this insightful book will serve you for a lifetime as a foundational guide for navigating your 'inner landscape' and approaching your tendencies, your light and shadow sides, and your relationships with compassion, curiosity, and a sense of humor. *The Seven Ways of Ayurveda* reminds us that we already have everything we need to thrive."

—JENNIFER KURDYLA (VATA), coauthor of *Root & Nourish: An Herbal Cookbook for Women's Wellness*

"*The Seven Ways of Ayurveda* is a warmly written, accessible book that teaches you to use Ayurveda as a lens for self-examination. Not only does Kucera kindly guide you to greater self-knowledge, she also gives you tools to understand both yourself and others in the office, in relationships, and at various stages of life. I highly recommend it!"

—SAGE ROUNTREE (PITTA), PhD, E-RYT 500, author of *The Professional Yoga Teacher's Handbook* and co-owner of Carolina Yoga Company

"Although we humans have a lot in common, we are all inherently different from each other, too. Sarah applies ancient teachings from Ayurveda to provide a whole new way to observe why we do what we do. A great read for people looking to understand themselves—and fellow humans—better!"

—HEATHER GRZYCH (VATA-KAPHA), Ayurveda practitioner and author of *The Ayurvedic Guide to Fertility*

The
Seven Ways
of
AYURVEDA

ALSO BY SARAH KUCERA

The Ayurvedic Self-Care Handbook

The
Seven Ways
of
Ayurveda

Discover Your Dosha, Tap Into
Your Strengths—and Thrive
in Work, Love, and Life

SARAH KUCERA, DC, CAP

THE EXPERIMENT

NEW YORK

For my favorite pitta-kapha

THE SEVEN WAYS OF AYURVEDA: *Discover Your Dosha, Tap Into Your Strengths—and Thrive in Work, Love, and Life*
Copyright © 2022 by Sarah Kucera

The Experiment, LLC
220 East 23rd Street, Suite 600
New York, NY 10010-4658
theexperimentpublishing.com

This book contains the opinions and ideas of its author. It is intended to provide helpful and informative material on the subjects addressed in the book. It is sold with the understanding that the author and publisher are not engaged in rendering medical, health, or any other kind of personal professional services in the book. The author and publisher specifically disclaim all responsibility for any liability, loss, or risk—personal or otherwise—that is incurred as a consequence, directly or indirectly, of the use and application of any of the contents of this book.

THE EXPERIMENT and its colophon are registered trademarks of The Experiment, LLC. Many of the designations used by manufacturers and sellers to distinguish their products are claimed as trademarks. Where those designations appear in this book and The Experiment was aware of a trademark claim, the designations have been capitalized.

The Experiment's books are available at special discounts when purchased in bulk for premiums and sales promotions as well as for fundraising or educational use. For details, contact us at info@theexperimentpublishing.com.

Library of Congress Cataloging-in-Publication Data available upon request

ISBN 978-1-61519-800-9
Ebook ISBN 978-1-61519-801-6

Cover design by Beth Bugler
Text design by Jack Dunnington

Manufactured in the United States of America

First printing May 2022
10 9 8 7 6 5 4 3 2 1

Contents

Introduction

People who know me now would never believe that I was very shy as a child. Painfully shy. I remember riding to first grade in the passenger seat of our white 1983 GMC S-15 Jimmy, hoping to convince my mom I couldn't go to school that day because I felt queasy. I wasn't pulling a Ferris Bueller—it was a real, visceral feeling I'd get knowing I'd have to interact with others, or worse, be called on to speak in class. I was only seven years old, but the sensation still lives inside me.

For many years, I saw my shyness as a flaw. It held me back from meeting new people, prevented me from asking for help, and made things like calling in a take-out order a most daunting task. But now, I see it as my superpower. Without that foundation, the traits that I love most about myself may never have developed. The result of my growing up shy meant that I spent less time and energy talking, which allowed for more space to watch and listen. Though there were hints of self-consciousness peppered in, overall, this provided a perfect opportunity to develop self-awareness, something that, along with time and the study of Ayurveda, fostered my ability to know myself well and to see others as their truest selves.

On my first day of Ayurveda school, our teacher and revered Ayurvedic physician, Dr. Vasant Lad, who was, at the time, in his late sixties, sat cross-legged on the carpeted floor as he conducted health assessments for each student while the entire class looked on. As new students, we were all eager to begin learning about Ayurveda—an alternative medicine based on nature and the five elements—and how we would be able to incorporate this holistic form of healing into our own lives. The first to take a turn was a student in her forties who, from the outside, looked happy and healthy. But after assessing her eyes, tongue, and pulse, Dr. Lad suggested that she seemed depleted. He asked her if she had been suffering from a broken heart. Tears began to stream down her face, as she nodded in confirmation. Her husband had died in a helicopter crash only a few years prior and she was still healing from this loss. The entire class was in awe of Dr. Lad's skills of perception, which only seemed to get deeper as he interviewed more of us.

While it's true that Dr. Lad's intuition is incomparable, his knowledge of Ayurveda provided fertile ground for his innate skills of perception to flourish to an even greater degree. Whether it was an emotional event that someone had stuffed deep down inside or a quality about themselves they hadn't yet come to realize, he saw not just our physical symptoms but who we truly were. I was so inspired by his ability to effortlessly and gracefully uncover what made each of us unique that I became determined to do the same.

I went into Ayurveda with the belief that I was embarking on an educational journey in nature's medicine that would bridge my chiropractic and yogic studies. I pictured myself broadening my scope of practice to include conditions outside of disc herniations and frozen shoulders and learning interpersonal skills that would enhance the level of care I provided not only my patients, but also my students, friends, and family. (I also fantasized about concocting herbal remedies from plants I had foraged in my backyard.)

While I did, in fact, whip up some medicinal teas and balms in my kitchen, by far, the greatest gift that Ayurveda has given me is the feeling of being understood. At the core of Ayurveda is an understanding that we are all made up of the same materials—the five elements, which are ether (space), air, fire, water, and earth—and how we look, think, and feel can be traced back to our unique proportion of those elements at any given time. This elemental makeup is the essence of our *dosha*, or the true essence of us. Knowing our dosha, or expression of elements, reveals the reasons for our inner thoughts, mental and behavioral patterns, and the way we interact with the world.

Thanks to Ayurveda, I can usually identify someone's elemental makeup in a few minutes through their physical traits and mannerisms. This information then gives me the insight I need to effectively communicate with them, imagine the sources of harmony and strife in their work and relationships, and have a strong sense of how they find fulfillment in life. And if given an opportunity to interact with them more, such as in an Ayurvedic consultation, I can see the connection between these attributes and their overall health, which is key in my role as a health care practitioner.

I believe when we embody the knowledge of the doshas, we recognize our superpowers and fall in love with the person we are. We can also recognize the superpowers of others and how we can offer them more support and compassion and interact in harmonious ways. If knowing my dosha can do this for me—and make me feel empowered by my shyness instead of ashamed—there's a pretty good chance it can open your world in the same way. But remember, being on this path requires patience, as self-awareness is always a work in progress. This process is about betterment, not perfection, and each layer of yourself that's revealed, whether it's one you're excited to uncover or not, fosters learning and growth. You'll find the real goodness doesn't come from reaching an absolute state of self-awareness but rather lies within the process of peeling back the layers. This book is about that very process.

A Brief Overview of Ayurveda

Ayurveda is many things. It's known as yoga's sister science and the science of life, from the Sanskrit words *ayus* (life) and *veda* (science). Ayurveda is a medical system from India with origins dating back thousands of years. While something created so long ago could be at risk of becoming outdated, Ayurveda has become refined because of its age, proving its knowledge is timeless. Ayurveda's foundation in nature accounts for much of this, as nature's rhythms are reliable and consistent. These roots have given Ayurveda strength to weather and embrace nearly any change or application, be it the corner of the world where it's practiced or the modernization of society.

On a meta level, it's no surprise that a system built on cycles, on change itself, is so adaptable, and we see this function-form relationship in Ayurveda's tools. In a nutshell: Daily, nightly, and seasonal rituals help people manage complex problems in simplified ways. Based on the rhythms of our bodies and nature, practices like seasonal eating, choosing consistent sleep times, and prioritizing digestive health can serve as the foundation for healing. These same concepts shine in the area of preventive health, offering dietary and lifestyle recommendations that take every person's unique makeup, or dosha, into consideration. This is possible when cycles are predictable and we can foresee the illnesses that stem from them.

To put it boldly, Ayurveda ascribes cyclical causality to everything: your craving for popcorn, why you get a sinus infection every spring, and the reason group projects work better with certain people. When you learn about yourself from an Ayurvedic perspective, you can't help but act with more mindfulness around how your choices will interact with the cycle you're in. This insight makes it difficult to arbitrarily choose a meal from a menu, to discount that the weather and seasons can bring on specific illnesses, or to disregard the shifts in the way we feel and how they may be related to our lifestyle. Ayurveda has so much for us to contemplate, and it rolls out an expansive path for endless self-evolution.

The Doshas: Ayurveda's Constant

In part 1 of this book, you'll be introduced to a few more of the fundamental concepts upon which this cycle-based approach to life is built. Where we'll focus most of our energy, though, are the doshas—the combinations of elements that make us who we are. Each of the three doshas is composed of two elements: vata (ether and air), pitta (fire and water), and kapha (water and earth). We contain all the doshas, as they relate to human biology and govern functions of our body and mind, yet we may find we have more or less of one or two. That dominant single or dual-dosha combination (you can also be tridoshic, but we'll get to that later) characterizes who you are, most of the time. (As you'll also learn about Ayurveda, nothing is ever really fixed or absolute, even your dosha! But it comes close.)

From the three doshas, there are seven possible combinations or expressions based on the degree to which each is represented in you:

vata, pitta, kapha, vata-pitta, pitta-kapha, vata-kapha, and tridoshic (having equal parts vata, pitta, and kapha)

Within this first part, you'll get a chance to take a dosha quiz to help you determine your inherent constitution. Keep in mind, though, that the results of your quiz are not sealing your fate. The quiz is an entry point into helping you think about what elements are dominant in you, and so it's only the beginning of your journey toward self-awareness.

In part 2, you'll get to meet each dosha or doshic combination up close and personal. Since everyone is made up of all of the doshas in varying amounts, there will be components from each of the seven doshic combinations you can relate to. There are self-study prompts sprinkled throughout to help you with this, in addition to sections about bringing balance to the doshas—a concept that can also apply to everyone. By spending time with each of the seven constitutions' mental strengths and struggles, communication styles, stress responses, and motivations and fears, you'll likely be more certain of your dosha and will be able to identify others' doshas, too. Bear in mind that you're not necessarily looking for a perfect fit but rather a best fit—which has as much to do with your gut feeling about your dosha as it does your knowledge. Additionally, reading about the doshas you resonate with least will bring more clarity to those you do most.

If knowing your dosha is a kind of superpower, part 3 will help you use your power to improve your overall health and well-being, as well as enhance your family, work, and love relationships. What happens when doshas interact can be a tricky—but fascinating—dance to observe, but knowing the qualities of all of the combinations will help you navigate these scenarios with more grace. To that end, part 4 contains advice for each dosha to thrive—how to care for yourself and support those you love—so that we can truly "see" each other.

In the appendix, you'll also find charts that help to give a snapshot of the doshas: their general characteristics and relevant details about how they affect the different aspects of life discussed in part 3. Use these charts as a quick reference and to help you see the parallels in each dosha's qualities as you meet them in these different environments.

A NOTE ON PHYSICAL ATTRIBUTES

It's essential to note that, while physical attributes are an important aspect of our dosha, this book highlights the effects of the doshas on our psychology. This isn't because the physical components are less important (in fact, physical and mental health are dependent upon each other) but, in an effort to highlight mental attributes, you'll find our discussion on the physical to be limited. This will help prevent you from molding yourself to fit the mental components of a particular dosha simply because you're a match for the physical.

Tuning in to our emotions, thoughts, and behaviors will reveal opportunities for awareness and growth, especially because many of us are less experienced or uncomfortable with talking about how we feel. You can see yourself in the mirror, which makes it easy to describe your bone structure, skin, hair, and facial features. Yet, when it comes to understanding how you typically respond to stress or knowing what your go-to emotions are, you may have to really think about it. Waking up to these parts of your constitution—your mental and emotional tendencies—offers limitless possibilities for improving your relationships with yourself and others. When you are ready to explore more of the physical aspects of the dosha, consider referencing my first book, *The Ayurvedic Self-Care Handbook*, or check out other books listed in the resources (page 235).

As with any discipline that asks you to look deep within, you might find Ayurveda rattles you as much as it comforts you. But such non-judgmental clarity is truly the key to thriving in all aspects of life—if you want to take five thousand years' worth of evidence as proof. If you glean only one thing from this book, let it be to observe and listen to yourself and others without judgment. Some of the things we struggle with are as ingrained in us as our bone structure, so there's little use in spending our lives wishing them away. But those aspects—like being the shy girl on the playground, who also happened to be cheerful and good at making others laugh—are also what give rise to our strengths and our ability to shine.

PART 1

Your True Nature

CHAPTER 1

The Fundamentals of Ayurveda

An extensive background in Ayurveda isn't necessary to use the doshas as a guide to life, but an exploration of the foundational concepts is. This isn't just for comprehension's sake; it's also to preserve Ayurveda's essence. Ayurveda is a rich and ancient system, and while we can independently draw upon specific parts and pieces—such as exploring the way our dosha influences our work, love, and life, without necessarily diving into food and hygienic routines—it's still best to see the system as a whole. If you're already a student of Ayurveda, this will serve as a refresher course for you. If you're brand-new to Ayurveda, go slow. Many of these concepts take time to understand, and it's normal to feel a little lost before you find your way. To learn more about Ayurveda beyond the doshas, the resources section (page 235) has a list to help you explore.

The Macrocosm-Microcosm Continuum

Ayurveda's most foundational principle situates our existence, including our dosha(s), in nature with a concept known as the macrocosm-microcosm continuum. This principle states that we (the microcosm) are mini models of the universe (the macrocosm), and that anything happening outside of us is also happening within us. The rhythm of each day, the seasons, the moon, and more all play a role in how we feel, think, and behave. And we're not only influenced by nature—we *are* nature. The same five elements we find in the air, sun, trees, rocks, and water can also be found within us (and in other animals, too!).

Every concept in Ayurveda is built upon this idea, so knowing it makes other Ayurvedic principles easier to comprehend. It can also create radical shifts in our awareness and well-being. First, accepting our oneness with nature will make us more apt to readily observe what's happening outside of us in our environment. We become more aware of the weather, the lighting in our office, or the volume of the music playing in restaurants and retail stores. This may seem trivial, but it's actually essential training for working with your (and others') doshas. This external awareness can then blossom into our ability to see the relationship between macrocosm and microcosm. Perhaps the fiery and passionate side of you might relate to the radiant energy of the sun, the fluctuations of your mind are similar to the gusty wind, or maybe there's a correlation between brain fog and cloudy, overcast days. The connection isn't always one-to-one, but it's a good place to start. In the end, the more connected to nature we feel, the greater awareness we have of ourselves and our relationship to nature.

The Five Elements

In observing the macrocosm, you may realize that there's some overlap within all the microcosms of nature's creations. Ayurveda explains this through the five elements—ether (space), air, fire, water, and earth—which are present in all life in different proportions. These elements are the building blocks of nature, and since they account for both our physical and mental makeup, they are essential in fully grasping the concept of dosha.

All five elements are found in everything and in everyone, as they are all necessary for living things to exist. We need space to expand and contain, air to breathe and move, fire to transform and understand, water to hydrate and flow, and earth to nourish and stabilize. However, each of us has a varying amount and expression of each element. This is why you might describe someone as *spacey* and another as *fiery*, and why being around one person can feel uplifting while someone else makes you feel more grounded. You may not have realized it or known exactly why until now, but you can already detect which element is most prominent in someone. In fact, you've likely used the elements to talk about their personality traits and the interactions you have with them.

YOUR INNER LANDSCAPE

If you're struggling to see how the elements are expressed in different ways, take a look at nature's landscapes. The desert, mountains, and coastal beaches all contain sun, water, and earth, yet it's clear that these elements are present in varying amounts. Determining which elements are expressed most in you is a lot like asking what your inner landscape is like. Are you the hot and dry desert, the cool and stable mountains, or the warm and watery coast? What qualities of the landscape do you relate to the most? Keep your answers in mind as you learn about the twenty attributes and how they are used to describe the five elements and the functions of your body and mind.

The Twenty Attributes

We might think it's easy to describe the elements, since we know them so closely, but Ayurveda loves to be specific, so it offers twenty designated attributes to describe the elements. And since you are made of the elements, these attributes aren't just describing the elements; they are describing you. These basic descriptors, called *gunas*, are presented as ten pairs of opposites (or imagine ten continuums): heavy/light, dull/sharp, cold/hot, oily/dry, smooth/rough, dense/liquid, soft/hard, static/mobile, subtle/gross, clear/cloudy. Given these continuums, we know nothing is one attribute or the other (such as hot *or* cold, or dry *or* oily); everything is both. Cinnamon and jalapeños both add spice, so they're closer to the "hot" end of the continuum. The level of heat varies between the two—cinnamon is less spicy than a jalapeño—but the heat attribute is still present in each.

Because the attributes are also words used in your everyday vernacular, you'll not only find you can easily apply them to how you feel, but that they also make the elements and doshas more relatable. For example, fire is the only element that is described as sharp. You might be able to deduce whether or not you have a lot of fire compared to the other elements, but it's ultimately because you are aware of the sharp, fiery qualities you have, such as a *sharp intellect* or a *sharp tongue*.

Even if this specific example doesn't resonate with you, I imagine you've experienced *rough* times and *hard* times, that you've had days where your mind was *clear* and others when it was *cloudy*, that you've been in situations that caused a *heavy* heart, and that you have felt relief when problems were *smoothed* over. When you're aware how these simplistic words align with your feelings, moods, emotions, and experiences, you'll become skilled at linking them, and yourself, to the elements and doshas.

Now, let's explore the gunas for each element in more detail and how these properties might manifest in you.

Ether

light, dry, cold, clear, subtle

Ether is the most expansive and infinite element. It contributes to the limitless qualities of your mind and emotions and brings forth themes of creativity, freedom, possibility, and potential. It's ether that causes you to be spontaneous and full of ideas. It helps you thrive in the beginning stages of projects, stand in your individuality, seek freedom from structure and schedules, and live for coloring outside the lines. Still, the light, cold, and dry attributes can also present as traits we struggle with: insecurity, fear, spaciness, nervousness, loneliness, worry, and the feeling of being unsettled.

Air

mobile, light, dry, hard, rough, cold, clear, subtle

Air facilitates mental movement and encourages us to make shifts and change direction. While air has similar attributes to ether, it has one outstanding quality: mobility. In our mind, air is like the wind: active, exciting, fast. It causes us to be quick thinkers, have rapid responses, be lively, and crave new experiences and variety. These characteristics can have less-desirable counterparts, similar to ether's—worry, fear, insecurity, or loneliness—and the presence of the mobile quality seems to only amplify them. This quality can easily turn expansiveness into instability, an abundance of ideas into a restless mind, quick energy into depletion, and a desire for spontaneity into a lack of structure. It's akin to turning on a fan to its highest speed with stacks of papers sitting on the desk, making your mind very scattered.

Fire

hot, sharp, light, dry, subtle

Fire is the element of transformation. It sparks our passions, transmutes thought into action, and turns our food into fuel. This element is responsible for motivating you, sharpening your intellect and emotions, and giving you leadership skills. When you have fire in your mind, your goals are on point, your to-do list is full, and you have a drive that's as intense as the sun is radiant. These fiery attributes drive productivity and accomplishments, but they also fuel anger, frustration, resentment, irritability, burnout, and an unhealthy need to be in control.

Water

heavy, oily, soft, smooth, dull, liquid

Water doesn't just hydrate you—it also enhances your fluid nature, making it easier to adapt to change (which is part of nature) and "go with the flow" without too much discomfort or drama. Water isn't as fixed as earth, but you won't find it to have the same ease with movement as air because of its heaviness. That heaviness means water is stable and powerful, despite also being soft and fluid. When these properties become integrated into your mind and emotions, they give rise to patience, understanding, loyalty, dedication, stability, endurance, and a deep sense of care. When the element of water hinders us in thought, emotion, and behavior, it shows up as sadness, a heavy heart, a sluggish mind, stubbornness, lack of motivation, and dulled thinking.

Earth

heavy, oily, soft, smooth, dull, dense, cloudy, gross, static, cool

Earth keeps us grounded and calm in unsettling times, as it has the title of being the heaviest and most static of the elements. While we do want to have mobility in our mind, this static element is essential in providing steadiness, support, and structure. The more earth element you have, the more secure and grounded you feel, which is good until it's so abundant you feel stuck, attached, depressed, withdrawn, and averse to change. If you're an earthy person, you may always need to keep these emotions in check, but when earth works in your favor, people will describe you as calm, easygoing, compassionate, honest, nurturing, and caring.

In the next section, you'll learn that two elements make up each of the three doshas. Since the doshas have Sanskrit names, you may find yourself referring back to the elements to help you better understand them. Rather than using both elements to name a dosha, we can refer to the primary element for each: vata is air, pitta is fire, and kapha is earth (the other element is said to be the "container" for the dosha—what holds the element or is the medium through which it is expressed). You likely have a clear understanding of the elements and their attributes from experiencing them in nature, and since you don't need to think long and hard to know what space, air, fire, water, or earth is like, they may provide a more direct link to your dosha and your connection to nature.

IT'S ELEMENTAL

To enhance your experience in learning how the five elements and twenty attributes relate to you, think about the elements that you connect to most and where you tend to fall on each continuum of attributes. Use the following questions as a guide:

1. Which element do you relate to the most? The least?

2. When you are feeling your best, where would you rank on each continuum? Where do you place yourself now?

3. Are there emotions, moods, or feelings you experience more regularly? How would they be described using the twenty attributes?

4. Think of someone you know who embraces a lot of ether. How is their personality similar and contrasting to yours? Try this exercise for each of the five elements to see how the elements can show up in various ways in different people.

The Three Doshas

Now that we've reviewed the fundamentals of Ayurveda, it's time to get to our main topic: the doshas. Used to explain how nature is expressed within us, the role the elements play in our health, and the way we think and interact with others, the doshas—also thought of as "constitutions"—are a central theory of Ayurveda.

The three doshas each comprise two elements: vata (ether + air), pitta (fire + water), kapha (water + earth). And since the twenty attributes are used to describe the elements, you'll also find that the link between the elements, attributes, and doshas provides a

complete picture of how the doshas contribute to our overall physiology, especially how they play into our emotions, thoughts, and
behaviors. We'll be talking about doshas in two different contexts:

1. How the doshas determine our human biology (you'll find this
   in the next section).
2. The seven different expressions or combinations of the doshas;
   how they show up in work, love, and life; and most important,
   which of the combinations pertains to you (our journey into
   this territory will begin in chapter 2).

Together, the three doshas account for your biological makeup
and all the functions, organs, and tissues of your body and mind.
While there are other concepts in Ayurveda to fill in all of the
details of human physiology, the doshas cover most (because,
remember, everything is elemental!). Each dosha has a primary
function, specific organs that it governs, and associated mental,
behavioral, and emotional tendencies—the good and the bad, our
light and our shadow sides. So while your constitution is sometimes
referred to as a mind-body type or a way of categorizing your
personality, it is truly much richer, as your doshas are in charge
of keeping all of your body's systems up and running and how
you exist in the world.

To reiterate, like the elements, all the doshas are present in
everyone. Nobody can claim to be void of any. This means that,
just as we all have eyes, blood, and skin, we are also all capable of
being creative, organized, and compassionate. This is why it's vital
to learn about them from the biological standpoint first—you can
think about this, in music terms, as learning the notes (the three
doshas) before you learn how to play the scales (the seven doshic
expressions).

VATA
Ether + Air

---

light, dry, hard, rough, cold, clear, subtle, mobile

Comprising ether and air, vata dosha is the lightest, driest, coldest, and only mobile dosha of the three. As such, its primary action is movement. All movement in your body or mind—circulation of blood, joint movement, breathing, and neurological impulses—is thanks to vata dosha. (But though vata is responsible for movement, the structures and humors it moves are often connected to other doshas; for example, circulation of blood is a vata *function*, but blood is a tissue governed by pitta.) The vata dosha also governs your peripheral nerves, ears, bones, and large intestine. And with regards to your mind and behavior, it's responsible for spontaneity, ability to be accepting of change, and creativity (even if you feel you have only an ounce), but it's also why you worry or feel anxious.

PITTA
Fire + Water

---

hot, sharp, light, oily or dry, liquid

Pitta is made of fire and water, though it's most often thought of as the fiery dosha, given that fire is the element most responsible for pitta's primary function: transformation. The flames of pitta are what allow us to digest food and thoughts, what initiates hormonal shifts (such as puberty, menopause, and andropause), and what transforms what we see into a thought, feeling, or movement (vata is the movement itself; pitta is what converts a thought into movement). It enables the mind to convert thought into understanding and intellect. It also governs our skin, eyes, blood, liver, spleen, enzymes, and what's referred to as our emotional heart and brain. Your pitta dosha is what gives you your sharpness of mind, confidence, the skills you need to plan and organize, and the conviction you need to chase your dreams and stand up for your beliefs. It's also responsible for emotions like anger, frustration, and judgment.

KAPHA
Water + Earth

---

heavy, oily, soft, smooth, dull, dense, cloudy, gross, static, cool

The kapha dosha, made of water and earth, is what provides us growth, structure, and protection. With the heavy and stable qualities of water and earth, kapha naturally governs your immunity, adipose (fat) tissue, mucosal linings found in all tracts of the body, synovial (joint) fluid, and lymph. It's also related to phases of digestion occurring in the mouth (with the kapha fluid of saliva) and in the stomach (where the lining of the stomach is governed by kapha). Kapha also oversees the function of your entire respiratory system and your physical heart and brain. In your mind and emotions, kapha is love, compassion, and your instinct to nurture and care for others. On the flip side, it can leave you feeling stuck or sad.

See the table on page 221 for a quick reference to the various aspects of the three doshas. Notice how they differ among the categories and how you relate to each of the doshas.

Like Increases Like and Opposites Balance

Our inherent dosha, or *prakriti*, serves as our home base. It's the place we feel the healthiest and our strongest ability to thrive. Yet, there are times that we wander away from it, leaving us to either feel sick or not like ourselves. When we experience such an occurrence, we are in a state of imbalance, called *vikriti*. This most commonly stems from the accumulation of any dosha, element, or attribute—what could be considered a theory of "like increasing like." We are able to tolerate the small, daily dances between qualities, such as fluctuating between feeling hot and cold, light and heavy, oily and dry; these are like blips on our health radar. But when we repeatedly consume food, are exposed to elements, or experience emotions that produce these same qualities within us over and over without reprieve, we will ultimately fall ill—and typically with a condition (in either body or mind) that shares these qualities. This can happen with any of the attributes, though this concept may be easier to observe or understand through certain attributes than it is with others.

For example, if in a day you consume foods that are drying in nature, such as coffee, crackers, pretzels, and popcorn, you may feel especially dehydrated or thirsty. If you eat spicy soup outside on a sunny day, you may feel hot or begin to have a heat rash. When eating a diet of mainly heavy foods, like fried food, meat, and cheese, you may notice yourself feeling increasingly sluggish and heavy. If these circumstances continue for a longer period of time and/or are accompanied by more dry, hot, or heavy characteristics, the result will be more extreme. The person who feels thirsty will start to have dry eyes and dry skin, the person who feels hot may start to have heartburn, and the person who felt sluggish and heavy may begin to gain weight. Unless the situation is remedied, the symptoms will continue to complicate. This process is not limited to physical causes or conditions; it also extends to the mind and emotions. Physical causes can lead to physical or mental imbalances, and nonphysical causes can create imbalances within body or mind.

Imbalances of any type can happen to anyone, but you are most likely to experience imbalances in the doshas, elements, or attributes that are most prevalent in you. There's less room for error when certain qualities are present in higher amounts, similar to adding drops of water to a bucket that is already at or near full. Vata people are prone to imbalances that are cold, mobile, and dry. Pitta folks may see more hot and sharp conditions in their lifetime. And kaphas have a greater propensity toward illnesses that are heavy and static. Still, it wouldn't be unheard of for an airy or earthy person to have an imbalance of fire, or a fiery or earthy person to have an imbalance of air. Considering there are so many factors that come into play, such as the nature of our society, the changing seasons, and modern life in general, anything is possible.

⌔ SELF-STUDY ⌔

WHAT BRINGS YOU BALANCE?

If like increases like and opposites balance, we can use the theory of gunas to find equilibrium through activities, foods, or people that can counteract the symptoms we're experiencing.

1. What are some of the current practices you use to maintain an overall sense of well-being (meditation, journaling, wellness routine, seasonal eating, exercise)?

2. When you don't feel well or become awake to a thought or behavioral pattern in need of attention, what practices help bring you back to balance?

---

3. After understanding your current practices and patterns
   through the lens of Ayurveda, what are some modifications you
   could make in your daily routines? Consider the qualities you
   may need to incorporate (refer to page 24) and their related
   doshas and elements.

When it comes to illness, most of the attention is paid to the accumulation or increase of a quality, element, or dosha, but it isn't just a matter of what is building up; it's also important to figure out why. Ayurveda recognizes three major causes of illnesses or reasons accumulation might occur.

The first is when we go against nature or time, when we act in opposition to the rhythms of Mother Nature, or we fail to stay aligned with our own true, inner nature. Examples of this could range from wearing clothing that's inappropriate for the season to making choices that are inauthentic to us, like participating in certain activities as a child despite your disinterest, purely to appease your parents, or choosing a career path as an adult because of the societal status it will earn you. You can assign an attribute to the way these things make you feel—too light of a jacket in the winter and you'll be cold; frustration from doing things you don't want to do will increase your internal heat. The longer you withstand them, the bigger the buildup.

The second cause of imbalance is misuse of intellect, such as when you know you shouldn't stay up as late as you are, work as much as you do, or drink an additional glass of wine. This isn't to suggest that there isn't room for variety, spontaneity, or indulgence once in a while, but when it becomes habitual, mindless, or contributes to an existing condition, you'll see the effects accumulate.

And lastly, we are likely to become sick when we disregard our senses. In the past, our senses were a source of survival. Our ability to thrive relied on our being able to hear predators, taste poison in plants, or smell fire. If we wrongly interpreted this information, it could have meant teetering between life and death. Today, our senses are both over- and under-stimulated. We are overexposed to screens, electronics, advertisements, and "noise" in all definitions of the word. Yet because we access so much via our digital devices, we are also in a stimuli deficit when it comes to interactions in the real world. We much more frequently look at nature on a screen than actually embrace it.

Ayurveda helps us right these imbalances with well-rounded care that spans from preventive to curative. Irregularities in sleep, energy, digestion, mood, and skin—even when minor—are considered important and are addressed using dietary changes, herbal therapies, breathing exercises, yoga postures, meditation, and the components of one's daily routine (e.g., dry brushing, self-massage, and tongue cleaning). All treatment plans are unique to the individual and take their inherent dosha, their doshic imbalance, and the season into consideration. Ancient and inspired by nature, the Ayurvedic approach can seem very different from Western medicine; still, many of the foundational concepts will feel sensible and instinctive. This makes the integration of this medicine seem very second (or first!) nature. And as modern society and technology have pulled us out of some of nature's rhythms, learning about Ayurveda can feel a lot like a homecoming. As you begin to become more familiar with the doshas and how they appear in and around you, pay attention to what elements and qualities give you this sensation of balance, of becoming reacquainted with yourself, or of coming home.

IS IT MY DOSHA OR MY IMBALANCE?

It can be difficult to discern the difference between your dosha's natural tendencies and what might be an imbalance. Even in the best of health, we have natural fluctuations in our mood, mind, and body, making it tricky to know if what we're observing in ourselves is our inherent constitution or if it represents a state of upset. The following questions can be used as criteria to guide you in this process. Keep your answers handy, and reference them when taking your dosha quiz (pages 48–50) and as you learn more about each doshic combination in part 2.

1. Is your current state natural and common for you, or is it out of the ordinary? When it comes to an abnormal physical or mental status, like not enjoying your favorite things or people, chances are you're in a state of imbalance, even if it's manageable in magnitude. Meanwhile, if what you're feeling is common or familiar, such as getting anxious for an exam or a first date, there's a greater likelihood it's indicative of your dosha.

2. How did you arrive at this state? Is the way you feel a manifestation of exceptional circumstances, or were you just being you? When what you're experiencing is a result of your everyday activities or normal wear and tear (e.g., staying up a little too late one night, missing your workout a couple of days, or indulging in sweets on a holiday), it's likely you're detecting your dosha at play. Yet, if you've arrived at this moment either by actions that are atypical for you, a traumatic event, behavior that is more extreme than your usual, or an accumulation of less than stellar lifestyle choices (e.g., skipping meals, over-exercising, change in job, death in the family, or overextending yourself with work and personal responsibilities), what you're picking up on is likely an imbalance.

3. Is this feeling short-lived, or has it been sustained? It's true that even the littlest of bumps in the road can be considered an imbalance. Still, something that's only been present with you for hours or days isn't typically going to sway the results of a quiz or be called into question when deciding your dosha. On the contrary, if it's been weeks, months, or years of feeling poorly and there's been no shift or reprieve, this is most certainly an imbalance.

4. Do you find that what you are experiencing is easy to recalibrate? Sure, a small imbalance can be easy to manage—like chapped lips, some nervousness before a presentation, or a little fatigue after travel—especially if it's something you've become accustomed to handling. However, if finding your equilibrium has been trying or unsuccessful, it is indeed an imbalance you're working with and not simply a characteristic of your dosha.

Note: We use the word "dosha" when representing both states of health and being unwell. Moving forward, the term "dosha" will be used interchangeably with "prakriti," or one's inherent constitution. If dosha is used in any other context, it will be specified—such as when referring to one's "vikriti," or imbalance.

CHAPTER 2

Insight Into Your Dosha

———

We've learned that vata, pitta, and kapha exist in everyone, but when it comes to applying Ayurvedic concepts to our own lives, it's essential to know how much of each we have within us. A solid idea of your doshic combination will help you see the areas in life where you'll thrive and struggle, map out your needs for support and self-care, and dial into the possibility for more harmony at work, among family, and in all types of relationships. If you haven't had a sense of your dosha from what you've read so far, you'll know, or at least have it narrowed down to two, by the end of this chapter. There are a few possible ways that doshas are expressed:

- You may be **single doshic** and be predominantly vata, pitta, or kapha. To be a single dosha means you are still able to observe traces of every dosha, but the characteristics of one continually stand out more than the other two.

- You may be **dual doshic,** meaning two doshas are strongly expressed, and the third dosha is far less detectable. The dual doshas are vata-pitta, pitta-kapha, and vata-kapha. With these combinations, the two doshas that are most present are either equal or are near equal. It's most common to be dual doshic, a notion worth keeping in mind when reflecting on your own dosha. Chances are, if you feel like you really connect with two, insofar as you find your physical and mental traits to be a healthy blend of both or you find your physical characteristics fit one while your mental fit another, you're probably dual doshic. For our discussion, you'll always see dual doshas written as vata-pitta, pitta-kapha, and vata-kapha, but in other sources and contexts where there's evidence of greater predominance of one dosha within the pairing, you may see it written in reverse order.

- You may be **tridoshic,** possessing all of the doshas in the same amount. This is the rarest doshic expression, but at the same time, it's what most of us assume we are when first begin to explore. This is because we will, and should, see ourselves in all of the doshas. But when you dig a little deeper, it's often revealed that you feel only one or two of the doshas truly resonate. The tridoshic person is something of a unicorn, which is how it will be referred to in designated text boxes throughout the book.

Even though you'll fit into the single, dual, or tridoshic category, you are still unique. Your inherent constitution, or prakriti (as opposed to vikriti, which we learned in the last chapter means a doshic imbalance), was determined at the time of your conception. It's dependent upon many factors, like the health of your parents—if one or both were dealing with any degree of illness or imbalance, mentally or physically, at the time you were conceived, that goes into your genetic expression. The time, day, and location you were born, planetary alignment—of both the time of your conception and birth—also influences your dosha. While you can't plug your birth time and place into an equation to determine your dosha like you can to determine your astrological sign, signs are associated with elements and can thus cause a greater elemental expression in you. This ultimately also affects your dosha. The factors that go into defining your dosha can never be repeated or replicated, hence why there's nobody exactly like you now and there never will be.

At the same time, you're bound to encounter someone with your same doshic makeup, only to find that, while you have similar over-arching life themes, you are different in many ways. Perhaps you are both predominantly pitta and fiery in nature, but one of you is an orthopedic surgeon and the other is a corporate attorney. These are two very different professions, but both are competitive fields of work that require postgraduate study—two signature fiery characteristics. Or maybe the fire element is expressed in one person through their outstanding ability to plan and organize and in another through their strong leadership skills. The message here is that our dial may be turned in one direction, but we are finely tuned in our own individual ways.

Because I love to cook, I like to think of each of us as special cuisine with the doshas as our ingredients. Vata is the white rice, pitta is the protein—we'll use tofu—and kapha is the sauce. If you're a single dosha—let's say pitta—it's like having a meal that's primarily protein with a small side of rice and sauce. If you're dual doshic, such as vata-pitta, your plate is mostly rice and tofu with sauce drizzled over the top. And if you're tridoshic, well, you're basically jambalaya. So, what we need to figure out now is, what dish are you?

Having an accurate assessment of your overall constitution will take some time, and ultimately you may find it best to seek out the help of an Ayurvedic practitioner. Still, you can trust that this chapter will give you a start and every chapter that follows will continue to fill in the gaps. Here are a few tips to keep in mind:

- Stay committed to learning about all of the seven doshic combinations before settling on the one (or two) that best defines you. The upcoming self-study questions and the dosha quiz on pages 48–50 will give you direction, but part 2 will offer you momentum and give you confirmation.

- Because you are made of all the doshas in varying amounts, you will absolutely feel at least some connection to each one. Highlight, circle, underline, and take notes in the margins when you find an aspect of a dosha that you can relate to. This form of tracking will help you create a tally, so you can see how much you connect with each.

- We are looking for patterns, not one-offs, so consider how you've been for most of your life, especially as a child (when you had fewer influences that might be shaping your qualities). If you're making associations based only on how you feel in the moment, you're likely relating to your state of imbalance instead of your inherent dosha (refer back to pages 37–38 to help you determine the difference).

- Don't compare yourself to others, including your family. Rather, think about yourself and what's natural, healthy, or ideal for you.

- When assessing your emotions or mental tendencies, consider what your first or typical reaction is or has been. Do this instead of overlooking a go-to reaction or emotion simply because you've learned how to manage it. For example, if you used to be temperamental, that tendency is still a part of you even if it's been years since you've lost your temper. Kudos to you for being able to recognize it bubbling up and knowing how to diffuse it, but the point is that it can still bubble.

- Avoid focusing on what's "wrong" with you. Be as objective as possible, and offer yourself some grace. It's easy to only see what you feel are your negative qualities, and actually, those very qualities might be the most identifying factors when it comes to assigning a dosha. Just remember that for every dark quality there's an associated quality that makes you shine, so make sure you're noting those, too.

- Sometimes the way we view ourselves is skewed, so if you're stuck, think about what others might say about you, especially those who know you best. If we feel down on ourselves or have some blind spots when it comes to our own traits, we may not have the most accurate perspective on who we really are. This can cause us to answer quiz questions incorrectly or identify with characteristics that aren't a part of our true nature.

- Consider which elements and attributes (see chapter 1) resonate with you most. These concepts are less complex, but they are still representative of the doshas. Use pages 25–27 to jog your memory.

- If you need a quick summary of a certain dosha's qualities, head to the appendix (pages 221–34) for tables covering physical and mental characteristics, light and shadow sides, and relationships.

Before you get a complete look at each of the seven doshic combinations, how about getting to know yourself a little better? The next sections begin to give you a more granular look at each dosha. Here, you'll get a preview of each section while simultaneously learning about yourself through self-study prompts. Approach these prompts with some amount of objectivity, like a scientist collecting data. Try to avoid being judgmental, as there are no bad or wrong answers. If you do find yourself feeling overly critical, attached, or defining yourself by your emotions, consider asking a loved one to weigh in or simply step away from the process and revisit it another time.

Meet the Doshas

To "meet" a dosha is to know a dosha's physical traits, their personality, and the health conditions they are most afflicted by. What follows are the general categories in which we'll talk about these traits, which will offer a consistent framework to help you build a complete picture of what each dosha is like overall and the most common ways they present.

⌐ SELF-STUDY ⌐
MEET YOURSELF

You may know your inner and outer nature well, but it's important to have the details, like past experiences and various physical, mental, and behavioral tendencies and imbalances at the forefront of your mind while determining your dosha. Write a short description about yourself that includes both physical and nonphysical attributes. Think about how you might describe yourself if you were meeting a stranger for coffee, talking to a new health care practitioner, or having a discussion with a best

---

friend. Go beyond things like eye and hair color, and give details
about your bone structure, your muscle mass or tone, and the
size of your facial features. Write about past and current health
imbalances (both physical and mental) and any patterns you
might notice evolving throughout your life. Explain some of
your more defining mental qualities and any emotional events
that you've been able to learn from. Use this all-encompassing
description as a reference when you take your dosha quiz and be
sure to also refer back to it as we deep dive into the doshas.

Light and Shadow

Everyone, or every dosha, has their celebrated traits in addition
to characteristics they wish they could ignore or hide. In other
words, each of us has our "light" and "shadow" sides. These
different sides come as a package deal, since the strengths we
see in a positive light can also cast a shadow as our weakness.
For example, your love of change can cause you to be commit-
ment-phobic, your leadership skills can reflect an inclination to
be controlling, and your innate ability to be calm or grounded
can also cause you to get stuck. So as much as we might wish
some of our less desirable traits didn't exist, we really can't have
the positive without the negative.

Our motivations and fears flip the switch between our light and
shadow sides. When we are motivated to have new experiences,
we'll show strength in being adaptable and open to change. When
we are motivated by outcomes and productivity, we'll have strength
in our ability to focus. What drives us can lead us toward the light.
Meanwhile, our fears activate what's lurking in the shadow side
of our dosha—specifically the fears that influence our daily decisions. These fears, or perceptions, can create a consistent unease

and cause you to regularly modify your behavior, like the fear of missing out, fear of not being of value, or fear of upsetting someone. Your motivations and fears are also what contribute the overarching "why" in life. If you don't know what gives you your drive, ask a perpetual series of whys. Why do you want to travel? Why is showing up on time important to you? Why do you place an importance on what others think?

⌒ SELF-STUDY ⌒

STEP INTO YOUR LIGHT . . . AND SHADOW

List what you consider to be your top three attributes (e.g., hot/cold, dry/oily, mobile/static). (You can go back to page 24 for a refresher on all the attributes.) For each, give an example of a light and shadow characteristic (e.g., "mobility gives me light in my adventurous spirit but creates a shadow side in which I'm unable to commit"). Can you see a relationship between these characteristics and how your strengths and struggles can feed into one another? You'll read about the most common strengths and vulnerabilities of each dosha later, but using what you know so far, can you predict what yours say about you?

Communication

Communication is key for all areas of life. Knowing when to be direct, lighthearted, or succinct can not only confirm your message is getting through but also reassure you that it's landing well with whoever is listening. Each dosha has a preferred method for communication (e.g., written, verbal, or in-person communication), in addition to having a preferred style. Knowing this about yourself is helpful for relaying information, but it can also help you find a stronger connection to your dosha. Similarly, since there's always room for the recipient to interpret a message in their own way (which may not be as you intended), knowing their dosha's communication style can offer some safeguard against this.

∽ SELF-STUDY ∽
HOW DO YOU COMMUNICATE?

What are key elements of the way you deliver communication (brief or lengthy, detailed or general, direct or indirect, frank or sugarcoated)? What's your preferred way of receiving communication? Think of someone with whom it's easy for you to communicate. What are three things that make interacting with them effortless?

Stress

Practicing Ayurveda won't liberate you from your stress, but it can help you recognize and interpret your stressors and become more aware and in control of your stress response. While under stress, our nervous system is stimulated—specifically the sympathetic branch of our autonomic nervous system. This is known as our freeze, fight, or flight response, a physiological function that is present in all animals and can be observed when they sense danger; for example, an opossum will freeze or play dead, a lion will fight, and a bird takes flight.

Even though our daily stressors don't usually involve confronting a predator, our freeze/fight/flight biology is activated in the same way when we face danger. For us, it looks more like avoiding the stress as if it doesn't exist (freeze), going toward the problem and taking action (fight), or looking for an escape (flight). My teacher, Dr. Lad, used to give an example of the three doshas (vata, pitta, kapha) and stress reactions that really drove the point home. He said if the three doshas were sitting in a room and discovered a snake in the corner, the vata would scream and run (flight), the pitta would kill the snake (fight), and the kapha would stand still (freeze).

∽ SELF-STUDY ∽

FREEZE, FIGHT, OR FLIGHT?

If you witnessed a car accident, what role would you play in providing help? For example, would you panic and move on (flight), would you tell someone else to call 911 while running toward the vehicles to check injuries (fight), or would you stop and look to someone else for what to do (freeze)?

Dosha Quiz

This quiz below is meant to serve as a launch point, a first look at what your dosha might be. Admittedly, quizzes can feel limiting and overgeneralized, yet they still provide adequate insight and are a great place to begin. No matter your quiz results, it's important to read about every doshic combination to see which fits you best.

For each category, circle the description that best relates to you (your answers to the preceding self-study prompts can help). Answer as objectively and honestly as you can, considering how you've been your entire life. At the end, total each column. The one with the highest total is your overall dosha (e.g., vata 3, pitta 11, kapha 1 means you are pitta dosha). Should two doshas total an amount that is close to equal or one or two points apart, you are dual doshic (e.g., vata 7, pitta 6, kapha 2 is vata-pitta dosha). If the totals amount to 5, 5, and 5, you are tridoshic.

	VATA	PITTA	KAPHA
FRAME AND STATURE	Small, slight, narrow	Medium and proportionate	Stronger stature with bigger bones
WEIGHT	Thin or underweight, difficulty gaining weight, easily loses weight	Average and steady weight, consistent, not overly thin, not overly stocky	Slightly overweight, stockier, easily gains weight, difficulty losing weight
BODY TEMPERATURE	Runs cold, cold hands and feet	Warm to hot, rarely feels cold	Warm or cool, clammy skin
EYES	Small, darting	Average-size, focused, intense	Big, clear, compassionate
SKIN	Thin, rough, dry	Sensitive, combination (oily and/or dry)	Thick, smooth, clear
SLEEP	Lighter sleeper, sleeps fewer hours	Average sleeper, sleeps average amount of hours	Heavy sleeper, prefers long hours of sleep
HUNGER	Variable appetite, snacks a lot , can forget to eat	Strong appetite, can be irritable when hungry	Low to moderate appetite, likes to eat, but content with fewer meals
ENERGY AND STAMINA	Fast, quick bursts of energy, but can deplete quickly	Average energy and stamina, not too fast, not too slow, can push	Slow and steady, lots of endurance, doesn't like to push
MIND	Creative, active mind, likes change	Focused, driven, goal and detail oriented	Calm, steady mind
MOOD AND EMOTIONS	Excitable, adventurous, spontaneous, lively, fearful, worried, anxious, nervous	Passionate, motivated, fiery, determined, critical, irritable, frustrated, judgmental, angry	Serene, content, secure, compassionate, apathetic, depressed, sad, disinterest

	VATA	PITTA	KAPHA
STRESS REACTION	Escape or run away (flight)	Go toward the stress, take the problem head on (fight)	Withdrawal and rest (freeze)
LEARNING AND MEMORY	Quick learner, short term memory best, forgets quickly	Average learner, sharp mind, average retention	Slow to learn, great long term memory
WORKING STYLE	Best in short bursts, shines in beginning phase of projects	Very focused with medium endurance, outcome driven	Not a self-starter, but has endurance to stick to task for a long time
RELATIONSHIP STYLE	Has many acquaintances, makes friends easily	Has average amount of friends and acquaintances, many relationships are work-related	Prefers to have a few close friends, maintains relationships for a lifetime
LOVE LANGUAGE	Words	Gifts	Physical affection
TOTAL			

With the self-study and quiz results from this chapter, it's likely you either have your dosha pinned down or you're wavering between two. If the latter is the case, chances are they are closely related, such as deciding if you're a pitta or vata-pitta, or if you're a kapha or vata-kapha. No matter where you are, you are the way you are. You're in a good place, and there's much more to come!

WHAT IF I GET MY DOSHA WRONG?

I have faith that you'll be secure in confirming your dosha by the end of this book, yet you still have to consider what to do in the event that you've gotten it wrong or just aren't sure. This can happen when you're in the beginning stages of developing self-awareness in general, when imbalance has affected your self-awareness, or when the quiz questions used to determine your dosha ask about things you haven't considered before, causing you to do some research on yourself before you can accurately answer. The best advice I can offer, outside of visiting with an Ayurvedic practitioner, is to take your dosha for a test drive. You can do this in a very general way by interacting with the world as your dosha would, checking to see if it feels authentic to you. You can also be more specific by choosing three areas of your life to study and journal about, such as how you respond to stress, what motivates your decisions, or which things in life need to exist for you to feel whole and happy. Finally, when you choose to make changes to your lifestyle based on your dosha, make sure those changes are small and gradual. This is important if you've gotten your dosha right or even if you've gotten it wrong, so that you don't add unnecessary pressure and stress in your effort to change and so that you can be clear about what modifications are having an effect. If you make a small change and it seems like you're going against the grain and becoming imbalanced, it's usually easy to take note and revert back to things as they were, completely unharmed. And if after all this you're still feeling unsure about your dosha, you can always go back to the elements and their descriptors on pages 25–27. These are the dosha building blocks, and if you feel a strong connection to an element or quality, you can refer to the dosha it's linked to.

PART 2

The Seven Doshic Combinations

CHAPTER 3

Vata

VATA = ETHER + AIR

creator, multitasker, shapeshifter, individualist, artist
*(See pages 222–23 for helpful tables summarizing
vata's characteristics.)*

Meet Vata

Susie races into yoga class at the last minute. She tosses down her bag and rolls out her mat, but before she can settle into the space, she sees a friend walk in and hops up to chat with her. Their short conversation darts between talks of recent travels, weekend plans, and a new restaurant in the neighborhood before the yoga teacher signals them that class is beginning. Distracted throughout class, Susie checks the messages on her smartwatch every time the teacher has the students pause in low lunge, and when it comes time for seated meditation at the end, she has a hard time sitting still, fidgeting with her clothes, mat, and hair.

Unable to settle, she decides to roll up her mat and leave class early. As she's hurrying to get out and onto the next thing, she forgets her yoga mat behind.

Susie is a vata, the embodiment of the ether and air elements. Vatas are bubbly, lighthearted, and full of joy, creativity, excitement, and adventure. Often eccentric in their style and personality, they celebrate the qualities that make them unique. While they aren't afraid to be an individual or stand out in a crowd, they have friends as far as the eye can see. Their chatty nature and willingness to strike up a conversation with anyone they encounter means they make new acquaintances everywhere they go.

And since vata is made of air, the only mobile element, these people love to be on the go. Whether it's planned travel, a spontaneous escape, or simply the temptation to fidget, the need to move is embedded in their DNA. This mobility can also be expressed through an attraction to change and new experiences. Vatas are full of ideas, they love starting new projects, and they're always looking for new ways to make life feel creative and fresh—a spectrum of actions that span from changing careers to rearranging their living room.

This mobility makes vatas averse to schedules, routines, or anything else that can feel too monotonous or restricting. With their attraction to change and irregularity, they function best in bursts or intervals, both physically and mentally. And speaking of physical, you'll typically find vatas to have smaller mass, height, bone structure, or stature, although sometimes we see them at the extremes—e.g., extremely tall or extremely small. Their facial features are also smaller or more delicate, such as thin lips or little eyes. They tend to have hair that's curly, kinky, or frizzy, and their skin is naturally on the drier side.

When they have indulged in too much of the movement, creativity, and freedom that feeds them, they can begin to feel unwell. Mentally and emotionally, we see vatas lean toward a storyline of fear, worry, anxiety, and an inability to focus. This leads to insecurities that can interfere with their relationships, work, and general ability to connect with others. Their propensity for change and all things new means following through becomes challenging in all types of commitments. They start lots of things but can't nurture or complete many. Despite having many friends, vatas' relationships with depth and intimacy can be few and fleeting, resulting in loneliness even when surrounded by others. Physically, they are susceptible to experiencing conditions that exhibit dry, cold, rough, hard, light, and mobile attributes. These vulnerabilities lead to imbalances like dry skin, dry hair, osteoarthritis, gas, bloating, constipation, insomnia, and energy dips in the middle of the afternoon.

Light and Shadow

Ether and air can translate to strengths like being a quick thinker, having an expansive mind, and being adaptable and open to change. But most famously, vatas are creative, even when it's a characteristic that takes time to discover. This doesn't mean that if you aren't an artist, vata isn't in your constitution, as there are many other ways vata (and creativity) can be expressed. Likewise, you aren't unequivocally a vata dosha if you thrive in creative fields. Much of what can distinguish creativity in vata form versus in another dosha is in context, approach, and how high it might be prioritized when it comes to core values. For example, an artist may create in a way that is a pure expression of their mind. Unless they have been commissioned for a specific work, their product is a result of more free-form creativity—a creative outlet that is distinctly vata-like. Meanwhile, architects are also creative, yet designing structures must be accompanied by additional calculated work. The components of their work that require them to meet specific criteria or be within certain parameters so that a building can be constructed is a task that's much more attractive to and suitable for the pitta dosha (see chapter 4). And while both artists and architects may feed their souls through design, the artist may be more likely to feel the creativity at their core or as a singular attribute while the architect feels creativity either packaged with or secondary to productivity and construction.

As a dosha's strengths are tied to their difficulties, vatas struggle when they overindulge in change or misuse their skills for dreaming up new ideas and starting new projects. The vata dosha is driven by excitement and renewal. They are pulled to things that feel fresh over things that are familiar, even when familiarity provides the security they need to cope with their fears. This uproots them and limits their ability to stay collected and anchored, which is already more difficult for them due to the lack of earth element in their constitution. They can easily lose interest in jobs and relationships, especially if they're repetitive and don't offer excitement (having nothing to look forward to makes them feel trapped and anxious). However, if they go with their impulse to move on to something sparkly and new, it can end up being superficial. Incorporating more of the opposite qualities—depth and routine—can help them to stay grounded.

> **BALANCING VATA**
>
> Write about a time when you felt most settled and secure. Where were you, what were you doing, who was around, and how did it feel? Think of ways you could incorporate some of the elements from this moment into your experiences when you're feeling uprooted or uncertain.

Communication

The airy, light, mobile, and expansive qualities of vata don't only show up in communication and interactions—they're actually foundational to communication in general, making those qualities even more obvious. Sporadic and animated, vatas have a need for physical and mental mobility, which can be observed quite clearly in conversations. They are known to talk with their hands, have difficulty keeping eye contact, and tend to wander off from the topic at hand. Asking questions is their forte, but often their mind moves so quickly that they are onto the next question before they've received an answer to the first. They're also fast talkers (a manifestation of their active mind), so it's possible to identify a vata type of speech purely based on speed.

These traits aren't only reflected in how they deliver verbal communication; they apply to written communication as well. Their quick and active mind can cause them to omit important details or include incomplete thoughts, leaving it up to the recipient to interpret the message. So while vata may thrive in storytelling and casual conversation, they can fall short when trying to convey details or directives in writing.

On the receiving end, in all types of communication, vatas are prone to missing some or all of the message. The longer the conversation, text, or email, the truer this becomes. Vatas can have a short attention span and get easily sidetracked because they're lacking the water and earth elements that make things stick. Sometimes their long-term memory isn't the strongest simply because ideas float away.

I find it quite advantageous to understand the communication styles of the different doshas when working with Ayurveda clients, and this applies to vatas in particular. I've learned that it's very easy for me to get swept up by the airiness of vata, causing me to entertain their tangential conversations and wiggle in my own chair as I watch them fidget. Before I became aware of their tendency to be scattered and my tendency to mirror their behavior, it was difficult to get a complete health history, develop a comprehensive treatment plan, and feel confident that all the proper information was exchanged and understood. Now, when I recognize I'm starting a session with a vata, I take extra care to sit upright, breathe slowly, maintain eye contact, and feel my feet connected to the floor. This benefits me and the client, as my being grounded allows for a more well-conducted appointment overall, and it creates an environment that helps them maintain a state of calm.

Stress

A teacher of mine once said, "If you drop something or make a loud noise, you'll know who the vatas are in the room because they'll jump." So it's no surprise that vatas mimic birds, another airy creature, by taking flight while under stress. Stress puts them on edge, creating a constant state of panic, worry, and fear. They become frenetic and hyperactive, and their response is reactive, often robbing them of the time they need to properly assess the situation and calmly formulate a plan. When they feel a stressful situation arise, their instinct is to escape. This could mean exiting a room, leaving a job, ending a relationship, or skipping town for a while. And if they're not physically fleeing the scene, it could mean mentally checking out, such as choosing to avoid the situation instead of addressing it, discussing it, or doing anything that reminds them of the problem.

Already fast-moving, their world speeds up when stressed, making it difficult to concentrate, focus, or remember simple things, like where they put their keys. This compounds their stress—like increases like in action. Like a pinball, they bounce from the stressful event (running late for an appointment), to their stress reaction (inability to ground or focus), and into another stressful situation (missing their exit on the highway). This means that despite their desire to run away, the stress lives with them until they can stop the cycle and discharge it—through physical movement or exercise, but more so by learning how to slow and steady their breath, heart rate, and mind.

Aside from more significant events that would stress anyone out (e.g., losing a job or the death of a family member), one of vata's biggest stressors is feeling confined, restricted, or limited. Vatas need space and movement to feel like their natural self; without it, they'll feel inhibited. They could have the same visceral response to being trapped in a plane on the tarmac as they would if they were trapped by the confines of a schedule, had to sit still or wait (at the grocery store, on hold with a help line, for their dreams to manifest), or were told to color inside the lines too often (both literally and metaphorically). All these examples can make them feel like they're wearing a straitjacket, and that feeling of constraint is one of the most stress-inducing things they can imagine. Thus, movement is usually the best coping mechanism when it comes to vatas and stress: moving their body with exercise, moving their mind with creativity, traveling, or even being in an open space that offers the potential for freedom of movement.

I have a real fear of missing out.

I welcome change.

I love starting new things, but I'm not so great at finishing them.

It's easy for me to get distracted and difficult for me to stay on task.

I have trouble being physically still and quieting my mind.

I value the experience of doing something. I'm less concerned with my performance or the outcome.

I have difficulty sticking with routines or keeping a schedule.

I prefer to do things quickly and to get them over with.

Creativity is an important part of my life.

I can have difficulty making decisions.

CHAPTER 4

Pitta

PITTA = FIRE + WATER

*perfectionist, challenger, visionary, achiever, leader
(See pages 224–25 for helpful tables summarizing
pitta's characteristics.)*

Meet Pitta

Rachel, CEO of a management consulting firm, opens her email and sighs out of frustration. The presentation that her employee was supposed to submit to her by the end of the day still isn't in her inbox. She'll have to do it herself, which might not be the worst outcome, since she almost always has to make improvements to her staff's work anyway. She adds a note to her schedule to work on the presentation after her kids' violin and tennis lessons later this evening, since she's already overbooked tomorrow between her triathlon training and meeting with the real estate agent to view buildings for her next entrepreneurial adventure.

THE SYNERGY OF FIRE AND WATER

Pitta's fire and water elements may seem contrasting, as we use water to put out fires, but water can actually enhance and spread fire's heat. Think of it like this: You take a bite of your spicy meal, then rush to take a big swig of water—only to realize that your mouth has gotten hotter, as the water caused the spice to spread. Or think of the weather: Heat and humidity together are much more oppressive than dry heat. The elements of fire and water in the pitta dosha act in the same synergistic way. Despite all this, we most commonly and first and foremost associate pitta with fire: While the water is still a pertinent element for defining pitta (the heaviness of water keeps pitta anchored and gives it form, and the force of water adds to pitta's determination and willpower), it's fire to which pitta's physical, emotional, and mental attributes most closely relate.

Predominantly fire and water, Rachel is a pitta. A thriving pitta has their goals in sight and an ample amount of focus, confidence, and determination to achieve them—on time, if not a little early. Pittas are hungry: hungry for life *and* hungry for food. As the fire element increases one's fervor and fuels one's digestion, these people like to know what their next big project is and when their next meal will be. Being productive feeds the pitta soul, so they take interest in keeping their schedule full and their routines on point. Given their natural leadership skills, they are proactive when taking on responsibilities and are always looking for opportunities to organize, plan, and manage. They may lovingly be referred to as passionate or perfectionists, as this dosha cares a lot about details, results, and goals. Checking things off the to-do list is one of their most satisfying acts, but their to-do list is always growing. For each task that is removed, one (or two) gets added. Neither the quickest or slowest learner, and with average long- and short-term memory, pittas take the middle path on many things. But this dosha is not to be labeled average, as they are the most self-motivated, most driven, and sharpest of the doshas.

Pittas are usually of medium build. Their bone structure, weight, height, muscle size, and facial features are neither big nor small, but somewhere in between. The sharp, fiery qualities of this dosha appear in their chiseled cheekbones, defined jawline, and intensity of their eyes. Many pittas have fine or thin hair and are often early to bald or go gray (it's said that too much fire in the mind burns hair and turns it to ash!).

When the light of pitta shines too brightly, their shadow side is revealed—which is perhaps more like burning up than shadow. They become addicted to action and outcomes; achievement, goals, giving direction, and organizing all things give them a high. When they blow past their limits, the healthy pitta morphs into a fire-breathing dragon—one that is irritable, controlling, rigid, judgmental, hyperfocused, and overworked. It's a burn that pittas crave, but it's one that results in burnout and burned bridges, as it can be difficult for others to maintain relationships with people who are in love with success and work, and pitta's drive can intimidate and alienate. This inflammatory effect we see in the mind can also manifest in the body, as pittas tend to have the mental strength to cause them to force things or push harder. Meanwhile, the sensitivity of their body is no match for their mind. When their fire becomes too strong, conditions such as ulcers, diarrhea, reproductive hormone imbalances, acne, high blood pressure, and inflammatory conditions can arise. This dosha gets all the conditions that have to do with sensitivities or being inflamed.

Light and Shadow

Many of pitta's strengths mirror those that are revered in modern Western society. Our culture pushes us to do and be more, an ideal that lives in the center of pitta's wheelhouse. They have grit, passion, and tenacity and are willing to put in the time and effort it takes to achieve their goals. The fire element is responsible for sharpness of intellect in everyone, and since fire is present in pittas in the largest amount, we find them excelling in academia, business, or tech (or often whatever field is receiving the most attention and press at the time). Pittas are excellent leaders and have strong organizing and planning skills. Don't believe me? Take a vacation with a pitta. They'll have read every travel guide for your destination, made all the reservations, printed itineraries for each day, and packed their carry-on with anything you could ever conceivably need. (This is their idea of "fun," which their travel companions might not agree with.)

Since our culture places so much value on pitta's strengths, it can be difficult to remember that so many of these strong points have their vulnerabilities. In their efforts to lead, be successful, and be responsible, pittas can easily slip into behavior that is controlling and hyper-focused on outcomes, overlooking the path of destruction they leave in their wake. They begin to attach goals to not only their work, but also to their diet, exercise, and lifestyle, leaving no space for play (they see play as a reward, not a necessity). The fire extends to all areas of their life, a true reflection of how combining water and fire can cause heat to spread. And as pittas are very self-interested, they can be unaware when they become irritable, critical, and judgmental to the point of hurting others' feelings.

It's tough for all of us to look at our shadow sides, but it might be the toughest for pittas. Since they strive to be their best and do the most, it can be gut-wrenching for them to feel (or appear) weak or admit failures. Proud pittas don't want to let others see them in their most vulnerable state. So, for the pittas out there who might be unveiling their shadow side for the first time, remember that a lot of growth can occur when your superpowers aren't available to you and your vulnerabilities are on display. Shifting your perspective could make exploring this side of you like a project—the healthy kind of pitta project.

Pittas don't usually have trouble mustering up enthusiasm for getting things done, which speaks to the origins of their motivations. They are driven by challenges, knowledge, and achievements. Dangle the proverbial carrot in front of them, and they'll find the means to grab it and put it on their mantel for all to see. Their career is usually at the hub of their life, but their drive for outcomes shows up everywhere— they even like to learn in their downtime (e.g., they watch documentaries and read nonfiction books). You'll also find hints of this in their relationships, as they carefully curate a circle of friends who they feel can help them be better versions of themselves—people with obscure skills, education in different subjects, or unique experiences. And while they're most secure when they're excelling in at least one area in their life (they need this to feel whole), pittas fear devolving, failing, and showing up in the world without purpose. Many of their life decisions put them on a path of growth for this reason, but without adequate rest or checks and balances, this path also leads to burnout.

I once tagged along with a pitta friend of mine to Target on an errand. I needed some essentials, and he was specifically shopping for a vacuum and some pillows. While I understand that both of these items require more time to contemplate—a vacuum is a more

> **BALANCING PITTA**
>
> Consider a typical week. What percentage of your time is spent on something goal- or outcome-oriented, and what percentage is dedicated to play or activities you wouldn't consider "productive"? If the scale tips heavily toward goals and productivity, how might you either release some of these tasks or incorporate more activities that are fun or where the outcome doesn't matter?

expensive purchase, and sleeping with an ill-fitted pillow could cause neck pain or a headache—the criteria he set and due diligence he performed made his true pitta colors show. He inspected each vacuum from top to bottom, noting any features that might break easily or not be entirely necessary (why have it if it isn't truly functional?), and each pillow was tested, as he laid on the floor in the aisle, the pillows still in their packaging. To my recollection, he left the store without a vacuum or pillows, as nothing passed his tests. These pitta qualities, setting high standards and searching for perfection, can be as helpful as they are inhibiting, even when it comes to a simple shopping trip.

Communication

"Bullet points" could be the singular phrase to sum up pitta's communication style. They like to be clear and succinct. Their work conversations and written communications provide enough detail to guarantee there aren't lingering questions, but not too much that they risk clouding the purpose of their message. In emails, you'll often find they highlight, bold, italicize, or use bullet points to draw attention to action items or topics that are a priority. This isn't only how pittas communicate with others, it's also the best way to communicate with them—with direction and conviction. Anything less will strike pitta as weak or underdeveloped, and they don't have time for discussions like that. A pitta manager might tell their employees to call them when they have an action plan, as opposed to involving them in the brainstorming meeting. This fiery dosha's communication style can come across as insensitive or harsh, but this isn't their intent whatsoever. When this dynamic arises between pittas and other doshas, it's important to remember that pittas are more transactional than they are outwardly emotional—their attitude is to see the problem and solve the problem, not to make you feel good about the problem. Thus, it's easy to mistake their passion for other more off-putting emotions, but behind it all is a desire to make the biggest impact on the cause they care about.

Stress

Like all fires, pitta tends to be intense, so when a stressful situation arises, they suit up and get ready to jump into the blaze. Fight mode is their stress response, and since they like approaching their problems head-on, they own their confrontational nature like a badge of honor. Stress can feel like a challenge to them, and that's comfortable territory. It adds fuel to their fire, which empowers them. At times, they may (consciously or subconsciously) seek to live in a heightened state of stress because it can feel exhilarating.

Still, even pittas can get swept up in undesirable stress, specifically when they aren't in control. This is especially true when they find themselves in situations that are unorganized, poorly planned, or lack logic. They have strong opinions on how things should work and trust themselves (and only themselves) to get the job done, so when they have to relinquish control or go along with a strategy that doesn't align with their sharp logic, they become agitated. Reporting to a boss who is less qualified than they are, working to meet the demands of a client who has unreasonable requests or an insufficient understanding of the field of work, or getting cut off in traffic can all be triggers for a pitta explosion.

Pittas may work well under pressure, but it's best for them to avoid feeling like they are, themselves, a pressure cooker. Since their internal heat increases as stress builds, such a sensation is probable. Without the proper ways to manage stress or let off some steam, pittas can become short-tempered, angry, self-critical, and burned out. It isn't good for anyone to internalize stress, yet given their sharp qualities, pittas need to be extra cautious, because when they are stressed, anyone in their line of fire can be affected. The more they hold their stress in, the more inevitable it is they'll project their stress onto others (and the angry pitta can be scary!). Taking ten deep breaths before speaking or acting is the best advice for a stressed-out pitta. They should take care to keep debates healthy and minimal and to always be aware of their tendency to take frustrations out on others. And when all else fails, releasing tension with stretching (especially muscles we contract to guard or protect ourselves, like biceps, chest, hip flexors, and abdominal muscles) or letting off steam with movement that makes them sweat (a dance party in the kitchen would suffice) just might be the most direct route to cooling their mind.

INSIDE THE PITTA MIND

I always do my best and I expect the same from others. It's difficult for me to do things subpar.

I'm quite autonomous, and I prefer to lead or to be in control.

Challenges light me up. If you give me one, I'll show you what I'm made of.

I welcome healthy debate. I'm not afraid of confrontation—and will do what I can to convince others to see things my way.

I'm reliable and people often turn to me as the responsible one.

I'm self-motivated and disciplined, especially when working toward something I really want.

People confuse my passion with being intimidating or having a mean exterior.

When I look at the things I do in a day or week, all or most are based on a goal or productivity.

I'm hardest on myself, but I can also be critical of others.

I have a tendency to be competitive, and I'm especially competitive with myself.

DOSHAS AND TIMELINESS

VATA

It's more common for the vata dosha to arrive late than on time. This is a result of their sporadic nature and difficulty keeping a schedule.

PITTA

The pitta can be very punctual, due to their perfectionist nature. However, pittas are also often late because they are thinking primarily of themselves. They think their lateness only impacts them: They might believe what they are doing is more important (and try to cram too many productive things in before they leave), or that others can wait.

KAPHA

Kaphas often arrive early because they like to be leisurely. Cutting it close would mean having to rush and that makes them uncomfortable. If they are occasionally late, it's simply because they move slowly.

VATA-PITTA

This dosha will be punctual, largely because they fear the consequences of not showing up on time. If they happen to be late, you might expect them to blame it on someone else or something out of their control.

PITTA-KAPHA

Pitta-kaphas will arrive either right on time or just a few minutes late. They are trying their best, they just don't like to be rushed and aren't great estimators of time. Given their combined pitta-like determination to get things done, but their slow kapha-like nature, things always take a little longer, but they want to get through what they're doing before they move on to the next thing.

VATA-KAPHA

Out of a strong motivation to never let anyone down, the vata-kapha will be early or punctual.

CHAPTER 5

Kapha

———

KAPHA = WATER + EARTH

peacemaker, loyalist, lover, comforter, nurturer, giver
(See pages 226–27 for helpful tables summarizing
kapha's characteristics.)

Meet Kapha

Kathy looks up from her desk to see a familiar face and gives a welcoming smile. She's worked at the reception desk of a publishing company for twenty-three years and knows the name of every person who walks through the door. It wasn't hard for her to learn them, as she enjoys conversation with people and has the memory of an elephant. Plus, it feels important, as she believes being able to say hello to someone by name can brighten their day—and seeing others happy sure does make her feel good, too. Kathy catches a glimpse of the clock as she looks back down toward her work and notices it's time for lunch. She was supposed to return a few calls before noon, but she doesn't want to miss her break, not to mention the leftover cheesecake she brought for dessert. She pushes away from her desk, pulls out her lunch, and goes to sit in her favorite comfy chair in the corner.

Kathy is a model kapha. This dosha is saturated with the soft and heavy attributes of water and earth. Kapha is known to exude calm, so much that you might feel a wave of tranquility wash over you simply by being in their presence. They have compassion in their eyes and sweetness in their tone, and they laugh at all of your jokes. The earth element is especially present in their grounded nature and ability to remain even-keeled, but it also contributes to their reputation for being slow—it just so happens that they are better at long hauls than sprints. Kaphas like to do things in their own timing and at their own pace; yet if you're family, a friend, or if they have a soft spot for you, they'll go out of their way to see you happy. *Note: As you'll learn in chapter 8, vata-kaphas also have this tendency. But with vata-kaphas, you are always their primary focus, and they can endure discomfort to support you. Kaphas are less likely to go out of their way for you if doing so would be a big disruptor to their own comfort or equilibrium.* They are loyal and committed and these qualities shine in their relationships, as they maintain connections for a lifetime. Averse to conflict, change, and discomfort, kaphas are the peacekeepers, stable and soothing forces in the lives of those around them.

The earth element bestows kaphas with large bone structure, strong stature, big eyes, full lips, clear and radiant skin, and thick, lustrous hair. With the strongest immune system of the doshas, kaphas don't log many sick days. If they don't feel well, heavy, oily, or static conditions will get them down. Sluggish digestion, lethargy, weight gain, excessive sleep, and congestion are among their common ailments. If they disregard minor imbalances and go through long periods of giving into cravings (which tend to be for sweets), forgoing exercise or not providing themselves with the care they need, they become more prone to deeply manifested illnesses like diabetes, high cholesterol, edema, and obesity.

When it comes to thoughts, behaviors, and emotions, the very elements that allow kaphas to stay grounded can cause them to become inert and attached. Both water and earth are heavy, and when mixed together, they have a sticky quality that leads to kaphas getting stuck. Their aversion to change means they have a propensity for staying in routines, jobs, and relationships even when they are no longer a good fit and it's otherwise time to move on. In other words, the imbalanced kapha can get into ruts.

Not all kaphas are empaths, but they need to be conscious of the possibility of absorbing other's emotions or giving too much of themselves. When their interest in caring for those around them becomes a priority over caring for themselves, their compassion and loyalty can end up being taken advantage of, leaving them feeling more like a doormat than a support system. This accumulation of heavy mental energy can leave them with the blues and without spark, vulnerable to depression and sadness.

One of the few kaphas that I know is also one of my best, and tallest, friends. As kaphas do, he walks slowly and talks slowly (I once saw him walk briskly to cross the street and worried that there was an emergency). He is loyal to his friends and family, and though he has had many promotions over the years, he has worked for the same company for all of the fifteen years that I have known him. In addition to these earthy qualities, one of his favorite pastimes is reading, and this is both a point of connection and contrast for us. I have more air and fire in my constitution and have no trouble stopping a book and never picking it back up if I lose interest at any point. Whereas my kapha friend once took months to labor his way through a single book—one that he confessed to disliking but that he also felt the need to stick with until the end. This endurance and loyalty, even if to a book, is one that only a kapha could possess.

Light and Shadow

No one dosha has strengths that outweigh another's; however, kapha's watery and earthy attributes bring the most balance and ease to our overbusy, overstimulated world. They are a bright light in their ability to be calm and stable when their environment is chaotic. They are resilient and have the patience to see things through when others quickly move on. And their loyalty and compassion are admirable. They'll always be up for listening, making you soup, or just sitting with you if they know it'll make you feel better.

In first learning about the doshas, I was taught that kapha had the loving and nurturing attributes of a grandmother. This was easy to grasp, as I recalled small gestures my grandmother would make in her own efforts to nurture me and her other grandchildren. My grandparents lived on a hill in rural Iowa in a house with a long driveway. As soon as my grandmother saw our car coming up the driveway, she'd start filling bowls with candy and snacks for us. The array of wooden bowls filled with treats sitting on the table when we walked in always made me feel loved and taken care of. While you don't have to be a grandmother to be a kapha, these grandmotherly characteristics run very deep in kaphas.

It's hard to imagine that people like this would struggle with anything, with their unwavering ability to care for others while juggling their own responsibilities, but kaphas are humans, too, and they have their own shadow side. Their dedication can turn into an inability to move on, their contentment can turn into complacency, and their loyalty can transform into the inability to let go. And to add to their struggles, it's tough for them to get momentum to change on their own. Without others coming to their aid, it can be difficult for them to get out of their rut—and even move forward at all.

People of all doshic combinations have coping mechanisms in place to help them feel a sense of ease, yet kaphas take this a step further by making comfort and ease their driving factors in life. Never should this imply that kaphas don't work hard or that they are without enthusiasm or determination—but when you look at the motivation behind their actions, the end result of relaxing and enjoying the fruits of their labor is their idea of reward. This is why they avoid change, why they often have to be tricked into getting exercise, and why they'd rather be a homebody than a social butterfly. The discomfort in all of these things (or at least perceived discomfort) outweighs the reward. While fear isn't a go-to emotion for kaphas, they still have their apprehensions like everyone else. In fact, their fears are nearly the exact inverse of what drives them: They fear losing their comforts, sacrificing what makes them feel content, or having to live with the unknown. Plainly said, they're afraid of losing their earth element, which keeps them grounded and secure, and having too much space, which can make them feel uprooted.

> **BALANCING KAPHA**
>
> Think of components of your daily routine that you have practiced for most of your adult life. Are they still serving you and supporting your current needs or have they become habitual, reflecting your aversion to change? What are some small modifications that you could make that wouldn't feel too disruptive, but would be better aligned with where you are in your life right now?

Communication

There are two key points to remember when it comes to kaphas and communication: Their pace is slow and their listening skills are strong. In verbal communication, this translates to speech that has a soft tone and a steady cadence. This might sound soothing, like a lullaby or a skillful meditation teacher, but if too slow and monotone, it could feel dull. While this could make a conversation with a kapha seem long and drawn out, especially if a vata or pitta is the one listening, you can always bet that a kapha's words will be authentic and deliberate. This is also true of any written communication. It can take a long time for them to craft a letter, text, or email, but when they do, it's likely to be thorough and thoughtful. With their soft nature, they are open to sharing (though they're not chatty like vatas), but you'll find their compassion shines most when they are in the position to listen. Expect not only a kind ear, but also continued eye contact and genuine interest.

Stress

Kaphas are heavy and static in normal life so it's only natural for them to become frozen in stressful situations. They evaluate the discomfort of the stress, and if the fix requires too much effort and hassle, they'll sit with the stress and hope it passes. They'd accept help from others if offered, but, being the nice and compassionate souls they are, they don't like to ask for help if it might inconvenience someone else. All this stress can add up, causing them to become lethargic and depressed.

It's hard to believe that the laid-back, earthy kapha can be affected by stress at all, but while they can tolerate more than the other doshas before getting rattled, they are certainly not impervious. It does, however, take something a little different to get to the nerves of the kapha person. Their stress reactions typically appear as discomfort or unease, most often related to change or external pressures. They prefer to work at their own pace—they're often slow to start new things, unlike vata, who can't wait to do something new—and for things to be simple, predictable, and without confrontation. They can endure being pushed to work quickly and outside of their comfort zone in small amounts, but that doesn't mean they aren't aware or don't feel it. Rather, they're more likely to internalize stress than show it; this holding on causes stress to accumulate and show up in their physical body as weight gain, increased blood sugar, or high cholesterol. Instead of dealing with a stressor actively, they hope for it to passively resolve on its own. Since rest and withdrawal are kapha's reflexive responses to stress, they need help being prompted to socialize, exercise, and add vigor to their life. These uplifting actions are good for them, but it's safe to assume they may need to take a long nap first.

INSIDE THE KAPHA MIND

I value and require solitude and quiet time more than most.

I'll avoid confrontation at all costs.

I resist change and enjoy the comfort of my own routine.

I prefer for others to lead or be in control, but I don't like to have too many demands placed on me.

It's not uncommon for people to comment on my calm nature. Others feel more grounded when they are around me.

It takes a lot to rattle me, but if you make me upset, I might hold a grudge.

Letting go is tough for me, whether that means letting go of a family heirloom, an old receipt, or the memory of being picked on in kindergarten.

I look for the ease in completing tasks. If a task isn't easy, you can be sure I'll procrastinate.

It can take a lot for me to get going. But for what I lack in speed, I make up in steadiness and endurance.

I sometimes wish I were as outgoing, active, or involved as others. It's just not in my nature, but I'm OK with that.

CHAPTER 6

Vata-Pitta

VATA-PITTA = AIR + FIRE

performer, illuminator, enthusiast, innovator, first responder
*(See pages 228–29 for helpful tables summarizing
vata-pitta's characteristics.)*

Meet Vata-Pitta

Jeff is running late for his client's marketing meeting. While he's pretty sure he can still get there on time, he can't help but worry if this will reflect poorly on his performance. He doesn't want his client to think he's not capable of the job, especially since he worked quickly to find a creative solution to their problem. But he also doesn't want to speed to get there, as getting a ticket on the way wouldn't look good either. In that moment, he remembers there's a shortcut. He arrives on time and gives a detailed presentation with glowing reviews. It turns out he was more prepared than he thought. Though everyone else is confident in Jeff's abilities, he often struggles to have confidence in himself.

Jeff is a vata-pitta, an equal (or near equal) blend of both vata and pitta, best thought of as a combination of the air and fire elements. Vata-pitta is composed of ether, air, fire, and water, but thinking about this doshic combination specifically as air and fire (and the absence of earth) gives us a more direct line to its defining characteristics: sharp and mobile. This constitution possesses strengths of both vata and pitta, but with some variation, as the presence of these elements in higher amounts mean they interact differently. In the single dosha of pitta, the fire is so strong that the effect of the other elements (like earth) on the dosha isn't considerable. This is also true with vatas, which have a strong presence of the air element. But vata-pittas contain lots of both air and fire, and their interaction develops characteristics you won't find in vata or pitta alone. We see this in nature when a little air blown onto a fire causes the flame to flare, or when fire causes the qualities of air, such as dryness, to be more present due to the excess heat. Air and fire influence people in a similar way. For example, the air element lends to vata's love of change, so much that they may rush into something new without too much thought. When you add an equal amount of fire to air, or pitta to vata, there will still be a desire to change, but there will be a pause—the critical mind of pitta will want to weigh the pros and cons before making the decision to try something new. Similarly, the fire of pitta gives them a passion to lead, but in a vata-pitta, the added mobility of air can cause uncertainty. So while vata-pittas are still wonderful leaders, they may approach leadership with a little less confidence than pittas.

DUAL DOSHA MENTAL AND PHYSICAL PRESENTATIONS

Dual doshas can be a blend of the two doshas in both body and mind, but it's also possible that someone with two predominant doshas will show attributes of one dosha in their body and the other in their mind. For example, with pitta as a single dosha, the physical and mental characteristics will both reflect the elements of fire and water. But in the example of vata-pitta, one of the elements—air or fire—could be more present in someone's body or mind, or they might have a similar representation in both. A vata-pitta could present with stronger amounts of pitta (fire) in their physical makeup (average build, intense eyes, sharp jawline) and may have a better representation of vata (air) in their mind (thrive in the beginning phase of new projects, seek out creative outlets). Or, it could be the opposite, with greater amounts of vata in body (slight frame, small eyes, dry skin) and pitta in mind (full of fervor and strong leadership skills). This variability in how dual doshas present can make it challenging to identify a dual dosha on the spot and trickier to conclude that you yourself are a dual dosha—even though most of us are dual doshic!

Vata-pittas have a sharp, fiery intellect that's combined with the mobility and creativity of air. As a result, vata-pitta is our quickest thinker. This dosha is someone you'd want to have on your crisis response team, as they're able to react on the spot like vata but maintain the focus and composure of pitta. Their energy comes in a burst, as both vata and pitta are light and subtle in qualities, which means they may find themselves requiring more rest than they think they need or depleting faster than they want. Vata-pittas are more flexible and adaptable than the solo pitta dosha, and they are more grounded (from water, rather than from earth) than vata dosha.

They like to show their playful side, but they greatly respect rules, schedules, and routines. And vata-pittas love new experiences and adventures to the same degree they enjoy being productive and a valued part of society.

With regards to physical traits and physiology, vata-pittas have a blend of both doshas' qualities. This makes it somewhat difficult to predict if they'll present with pitta's average build or vata's more delicate structure and so on, but it is possible to anticipate their susceptibility to illness. Their physical conditions present as hot and dry, and they appear most often in their skin, reproductive system, digestion, joints, and blood. Some of their most common ailments will be eczema, irritable bowel syndrome, tendinitis, and waking frequently during the night with an overactive mind.

Mentally, vata-pittas overthink things, worry a lot about what others think, and can be prone to self-doubt. They often suffer from perfectionist procrastination—not starting something because they don't feel they have the ability to do it perfectly. This isn't unique to vata-pittas, as pittas are our token perfectionists. What's different, however, is that pittas want to do something the best they possibly can—either for ego's sake or just to prove that they can—while vata-pittas want to do the best out of a fear of failing, particularly in front of others. Don't confuse this with kapha's people-pleasing nature; vata-pittas typically seek to please others for external validation. They're also prone to burnout, as is typical of any dosha containing pitta. Vata-pittas burn out easily because they're interested in many things (vata) and have a desire to do all things well (pitta). This is the most classic case of vata's airiness "fanning the flames" of pitta. It can be easy to feel satisfied when there are only a few, targeted goals (more of a signature pitta trait), but when you're hungry for many, and always new, opportunities, it's impossible to digest them all, especially since the ungrounded vata-pitta sets very high standards for themselves. (As a vata-pitta myself, if there's one lesson I'm constantly striving to learn, it's this one. Trying not to pursue every interest or opportunity that arises and finding realistic expectations for those projects I'm already committed to takes major discipline and diligence!)

Light and Shadow

The synergy of vata and pitta bestows speed and perceptivity. Vata-pittas are discerning, proficient at quickly assessing situations, and crafty when it comes to finding fast and creative solutions to difficult problems. They have both an internal and an external awareness, so they can simultaneously be tuned in to their own feelings and the feelings of others. This can lead to a desire to strive for fairness in all they do and to be cautious that their words and actions don't negatively impact someone else.

Struggles arise when vata-pitta's quick reactions cause them to miss important details, lose steam, or abandon tasks before they are completed. Vata-pitta's perception of the outside world transforms into a shadow side that worries too much about what's happening with others, which can lead to crippling self-awareness or create a breeding ground for comparison or fear of missing out. Sometimes their concern for others is overly self-driven; they don't want their words or actions to make someone feel bad in fear of how it might reflect poorly on themselves. They can also lose themselves in their search for validation: Their air might blow out their spark instead of igniting it, leaving them to forget what they really love or who they truly are.

Vata-pittas are motivated by acceptance and, consequently, they fear abandonment. They are strongly driven by external validation, and when they have any reason to doubt themselves or a situation, they become self-conscious and insecure. They are talented and skilled, but the presence of the air element brings forth an unsteadiness that always makes them question themselves, especially when they aren't receiving any positive reinforcement.

For kids, the playground can become an arena for acceptance and rejection. This was true when I was growing up, as one's degree of fitting in was determined by the order you were picked by the team captain in kickball. Very cliché, but nobody who was anybody would ever be picked last for kickball. The only way to avoid being picked last, aside from being friends with the captain, was to be a kickball prodigy—which I decided was the only viable option for me. In the evenings, I'd ask one of my parents to roll the ball to me in the street outside my house, aiming to perfect a powerful kick that no captain could deny. This determination to be the best, driven by the desire to be accepted, is a classic display of vata-pitta fears and motivations.

> **BALANCING VATA-PITTA**
>
> Balancing Vata-Pitta: What does confidence feel like to you? What allows you to feel self-assured in your skills and abilities? When you are confident, how do others see you and respond to you?

Communication

When it comes to communication, we again have to consider how components of both vata and pitta interact to make the ways vata-pitta communicates unique. Quick-thinking vata plus detail-oriented pitta yields a communication style that is rapid and succinct yet still maintains clarity and precision. While the blend of vata and pitta has its high notes when it comes to communication, there are also areas in which to be mindful. Vata-pitta's propensity to lack certainty or confidence will appear. This means that though vata-pitta will relay all of the pertinent information, it may be accompanied by disqualifying statements or an indecisive tone, or it might take on a meek quality. For example, a vata-pitta's email may have all of pitta's signature trademarks—key elements bulleted and written in bold—but conclude with questions or statements with the uncertainty of vata: "if you have time" or "no rush," "depending on how you feel" or "if that's okay with you." This can not only cause the message to be diluted but also make the recipient feel like vata-pitta's commands or action items are optional. Vata-pittas want to be sensitive and considerate of others, but when this concern is taken to the extreme, their sensitivity can come through as insecurity—more evidence of the little earth element they have in their constitution.

Stress

In observing vata-pitta's response to stress, we'll see the flight of vata and the fight of pitta. This doesn't specifically indicate that they fight then flee, nor the opposite. Instead, stress induces a heightened state of mental acuity—focused but in a short burst—until an escape is needed. In other words, they readily jump into (and out of) action. This makes vata-pittas great in emergencies or high-pressure situations, but only for a short duration. The stress is initially exhilarating—it's a challenge that also makes them feel useful— yet when the thrill begins to wear off, they deplete quickly.

Vata-pittas also need to be seen and acknowledged by others to value themselves or understand their worth. If they're hustling at their job, feeling like they're outperforming their coworkers but not receiving recognition, it will trigger them to become tense and resentful. But if they're trying their best but don't feel they're where they should be, they will also experience stress. As such, the opinions of others can mean more to them than their opinion of themselves. Knowing someone likes them or approves of them can bring great relief—even a small injection of confidence goes a long way. If this isn't available to them, they can try to stop their stress cycle by writing out a list of their strengths or the attributes they are most grateful for or by going for a long, slow walk—a way to release stress through movement without the speed, heat, or intensity that would aggravate the air and fire elements of vata-pitta.

INSIDE THE VATA-PITTA MIND

Structure is healthy for me, and I can stick to a routine, but I also love the flexibility to be spontaneous.

I'd rather follow the rules than risk getting in trouble.

I am organized, determined, and most energized in the beginning stages of projects.

I can act quickly and with a clear mind, but I find my endurance can be lacking.

I often question my abilities and have noticed that others have more belief in me than I have in myself.

I find myself replaying conversations, concerned that I said the wrong thing and either offended someone or made myself look bad.

Even if I'm fully prepared or qualified, I still lack confidence.

It's not uncommon for me to feel like I'm not enough.

I worry a lot about what others think.

I have the ability to lead, but sometimes it's easier to collaborate or follow someone else's direction and ideas because I often doubt my decisions.

CHAPTER 7

Pitta-Kapha

———

PITTA-KAPHA = FIRE + EARTH

guardian, investigator, moralist, helper, observer, martyr
(See pages 230–31 for helpful tables summarizing
pitta-kapha's characteristics.)

Meet Pitta-Kapha

Ben is helping his daughter move to college, and since she won't be living at home any longer, he wishes there was more time for them to be together. He regrets that his work as a researcher often caused him to miss out on time with her, but even though he's passionate about his work, she is the reason he worked so hard. Reflecting back, he wishes he had told her this, yet he also hopes that all the times he took her to soccer practice, helped her with math homework, and fixed her car showed her how much he cares. As they unpack the last boxes and Ben turns to leave, he hands her a gift. It's his favorite flashlight with a note attached: "When I can't be here to keep you safe, may this light help guide you home." The perfect practical, yet sentimental gift.

When you blend fire, water, and earth together, you get a patient, devoted, and down-to-earth pitta-kapha, just like Ben. For this dual dosha, we see pitta traits like focus, sharp intellect, impeccable organization, and excellent planning skills, merged with kapha's endurance, care, and calm. Pitta-kaphas can sit and actively listen as you talk through your personal issues for hours; they can happily research a single topic or issue for days; and they can fix the unfixable, tinkering with whatever's broken until it works like new. They are thoughtful and compassionate, and they offer lasting friendship with deep connection. Known by their family as the reliable ones, it's natural for the pitta-kapha to be hospitable and willingly step in to help when needed. Remember, however, it's the vata-pitta you want to show up in an emergency and pitta-kapha to be at your side when you need help for the long haul.

Second only to kapha, pitta-kapha's bone structure and immune system are sturdy and incredibly resilient. Their physical features reflect the hardy aspects of fire and earth, including average to big size and some coloring in their skin, hair, or eyes that's representative of pitta. Regarding health and balance, pitta-kaphas should be aware that their fiery nature motivates them to push, mentally and physically, and their earthy qualities give them stability, strength, and endurance. It's like they have a beast mode, with strong determination or force *and* sustainability (like they could lift really heavy things for a really long time!). If they're unaware of these qualities, however, pitta-kaphas override any signals their body or mind may be telling them to stop. They might be physically tired, but their determination will allow them to push through—a point where other doshas would fizzle out (especially vatas or vata-pittas) and neither their body or mind would allow to carry on. Or they could be so focused on a work task or home project that they forgo exercise, sleep, or time with friends—components of physical and mental health that are necessary for any dosha to stay balanced.

Still, even this dosha can't carry on forever. When fatigue, frustration, digestion irregularities, and inflammation increase and go unnoticed or are ignored, deep sickness, such as cancers or serious heart conditions, can ultimately arise as if from nowhere. And as the combined pitta and kapha doshas and fire and earth elements are heavy, immobile, and hot, the pitta-kapha's body and mind have trouble letting go—whether it be a grudge, high blood sugar, high cholesterol, or weight gain. And since pitta-kaphas can be very internal, sometimes others aren't aware of their struggles. This means nobody, including themselves, is aware that there's a problem until it has reached a point where they become very sick—which, as a result of their stamina, may not occur until midlife or later. And in this scenario, they can be envious of the more delicate constitutions, like vata or vata-pitta, who become more experienced in managing weaknesses given that they deplete much faster and often encounter imbalances earlier in life.

Pitta-kaphas are silent sufferers, keeping to themselves when they aren't feeling well and preferring to handle problems on their own (they're lacking in ether and air elements, which make other doshas more expressive or verbal). So, when this dosha becomes outwardly agitated and begins to complain or pull people into their experience, you know they've reached—or even surpassed— their max. This isn't likely to happen often, as they are one of the more emotionally and mentally stable doshas, rooted in logic that's

> ### BALANCING PITTA-KAPHA
>
> What do you allow to accumulate? What emotions, experiences, or thoughts have you taken on and internalized simply because you felt like it was your responsibility to do so instead of asking for help? How did that end for you?

coupled with calm. But if they're experiencing imbalance, you can expect to see stubbornness, a pressure cooker–like temper, a jaded or negative attitude, or an uncooperative nature come through.

Light and Shadow

The pitta-kapha has the good fortune of having both brains and (mental) brawn, making their strongest attribute their mental and emotional fortitude. You'll witness this strength in the way they zero in on a passion project for hours, days, or weeks, unaware of the time that's passed and completely content being alone with their work. They'll get lost in researching and investigating—going down rabbit holes is their specialty. And when other doshas lose interest or deem a problem unsolvable, the determination of the pitta-kapha will prevail. The pitta-kapha stamina is one to covet (until it holds them captive, that is). And the same type of commitment and investment is present in their relationships. Not everyone will be in their circle of close friends, but those who are will be spoiled with their devotion. They may not always verbalize their love, but they'll be with you through thick and thin.

While pitta-kaphas aren't necessarily averse to change, they don't like to give up or give in, especially when a lot of time and energy has already been invested (which is usually the case for the things they take on). The more challenging something becomes, the more they want to stick with it—as a result of the fire (pitta) in their constitution. But when they don't look up from their work long enough to get a panoramic view of life (a view that includes unique experiences, new opportunities, and people who love them), they risk neglecting their own care and health. They need to refresh, move, and interact with others—activities that lead to integration of the space and air elements—to support balance.

Hospitality, ethics and moral codes, and solving the unsolvable are all motivators for the pitta-kapha. They have a desire to get things right and also to do right by themselves and others. The decisions they make and the projects they sign onto have nothing to do with external competition, impressing anyone, or earning outside approval; they're all about fulfillment and virtue. Their loyalty and commitment to a person or an idea gives them their focus and drive. I experienced this once while hiking with my pitta-kapha boyfriend. We ran into a work crew made up of college students doing maintenance on the mountain trail. I mentioned that I would have loved to have that job when I was younger and that I especially loved the idea of working outside and building things. "Me, too," he said, "I would love to be able to build something for others to enjoy." While I, a vata-pitta, wanted to be part of the crew for fun and to produce something *I* could be proud of, he wanted to create something others would value. Where a vata-pitta's intentions would involve more ego, a pitta-kapha is motivated to help and support others.

Opposing pitta-kapha's motivations is a fear of being put in a position that compromises their morals and values, or inadvertently causing someone pain or harm (or just being accused of doing so), despite acting with the best intentions. *Note: This is different from vata-pitta's fear of not getting approval, as the vata-pitta seeks external validation, whereas the pitta-kapha is afraid of their intentions not being actualized.* For example, they may put their time, energy, heart, and even money into doing what they feel is necessary to repair a relationship or to complete a project to the best of their abilities. Then, if their partner fails to appreciate their efforts and continues to point out flaws, or the client isn't satisfied and only gives criticism, the pitta-kapha will be devastated that they couldn't fix it or be of service. Given this example, you may think anyone mindful of their work and others' feelings could have this fear. In part, you'd be right. But this feeling is much stronger for the pitta-kapha, so much so that it creates a feedback loop between their motivations and fears. With each potential case of harm or disappointment (their fear), they work even more diligently to uphold their ethical beliefs and fix what needs to be repaired (their motivation), whether or not they're the ones that have broken it.

Communication

Deliberate and reserved in their communication, pitta-kaphas are people of few words. It isn't that they lack things to contribute or say; rather, they want everything they say to be meaningful. This is true of both their written and verbal communications. You won't hear them chitchat about the weather to fill silence; they won't ask how you are without expecting a sincere answer; and they won't use superlatives unless warranted. They can be taken for face value, as they are known to be straightforward— which might lead you to interpret them as cold or even a loner (remember that their lack of space and air limits what they have to say and could make them seem antisocial). Despite this, they are still able to effortlessly maintain kindness without sugarcoating things (contrast this with vata or pitta, who are more likely to be blunt and filter-less), and their speech is soft, confident, and nurturing.

Stress

While stress rattles all constitutions (that is the nature, or you could say, dosha, of stress!), this combination teaches us that it's possible to remain calm and think with clarity during some of life's most challenging times. When faced with stress, you'll see the pitta-kapha dosha pause, look at the situation from every angle, then take action based on what they've assessed. Their earthy instincts tell them to freeze; their fiery ones tell them to fight. For this reason, they are some of our most patient problem solvers.

Pitta-kapha people are very internal with their emotions. Thus, there could be a storm brewing on the inside—one full of pitta-like emotions, such as frustration, irritation, or anger—where all you see is their sunny disposition on the outside. Eventually, that slow-moving storm arrives, and you'll have the heavy rain and long rumbles of thunder, but it will be less intense than an electrifying pitta storm.

Pitta-kaphas experience the most stress when they're put in a position to act outside of their ethical parameters, against their greater intentions, or at a pace that isn't self-determined. More self-motivated than the singular kapha dosha and softer than the pure pitta, they want to be methodical and to do things their own way and at their own pace while still being hospitable and invested in the happiness of others. When their care and concern for the rights and well-being of others is taken advantage of, or when they are pushed to remedy problems faster than they would like, they feel stress. The intensity heightens if the same issue is pressed repeatedly, or if their needs aren't considered. Because the pitta-kapha is stubborn (like kapha), they don't like to accept help or admit to themselves that what they are doing isn't working (like pitta), so their stress cycle can amplify when they don't speak up or reach out. They can release stress and feel like themselves again when they're able to fully metabolize the stressful experience in their body and mind with an intense workout, vigorous breathing exercises, or writing a letter that they'll never send.

The more difficult a problem is, the more motivated I am to find the solution, no matter how much time and patience is required.

I prefer to take my time to produce the quality of work I desire, rather than work under someone else's timeline or create work that isn't to my standards.

I am comfortable in my ability to serve others while maintaining my own boundaries.

I am aware of and acknowledge my strengths and skills.

I have great mental endurance and ability to focus, but this can cause me to go down some deep rabbit holes.

I'm very internal with my thoughts and emotions.

I can prioritize the needs of others over my own, but not having my needs met causes anger to build.

It can be difficult for me to voice my concerns and desires until I've hit a breaking point, at which time I might erupt.

I like to be autonomous, but I don't necessarily feel a desire to be a leader.

I can be relatively reserved upon first meeting, but once I connect with someone and understand I can trust them, I'm very open.

DOSHAS AND TRAVEL

If we had to categorize it, travel is a vata-like activity, full of ether and air elements, given the movement and change involved (and sometimes literal air if one is traveling by plane). There's a dose of pitta (fire and water), as travel typically also involves planning, and often a touch of kapha, if the travel is for a relaxing vacation.

 VATA Vatas travel for adventure. They don't like to have a plan or an agenda; rather, they like to play things by ear. They're also known to forget some of the essentials when packing.

 PITTA You could think of the *p* in pitta as many things—planner, prepared, perfectionist, persuasive, precise—and all are relevant to travel. Far in advance, they research the places they want to go, which often includes something educational or historic. They have an agenda and it requires an alarm clock in the morning. Forget your toothbrush or umbrella? The pitta has an extra you can borrow.

 KAPHA Kaphas travel for leisure. Though they have sights they'd like to see, their rest, relaxation, and eating experiences are a priority. You can expect sleeping in, coffee breaks, and late dinners. Though this dosha doesn't overprepare and can put off packing until the last minute, they are sure to pack their comforts.

 VAIA-PITTA This dosha travels with a few things planned, but they also like to have options, as they are likely to change their mind in the moment. They like to visit some of the "must-see" places but also like some excitement and exploration. When packing their luggage, they'll forget some of the essentials but end up with extra socks and underwear. And when flying, there's a good chance they'll repeatedly check their departure time because they forgot their flight time or are worried they got it wrong and don't want to miss their flight.

PITTA-KAPHA

Late mornings and late dinners, pitta-kaphas travel in a slow and intentional way. While no real agenda is made in advance, they have one or two things in mind that they don't want to miss. The rest of the space can be filled with afternoons in cafés and culinary treats. Regarding luggage, they'll carry anything they feel they might want or need, and they'll take as much time as they'd like to pack.

VATA-KAPHA

The least likely dosha to travel alone, vata-kaphas are along for the ride. They're fine to do what you have planned—tell them what to bring and they'll come prepared, but they also want to have free time, either for their own exploration or for rest, throughout the day.

CHAPTER 8

Vata-Kapha

VATA-KAPHA = AIR + EARTH

dreamer, merger, supporter, sidekick, conversationalist
(See pages 232–33 for helpful tables summarizing
vata-kapha's characteristics.)

Meet Vata-Kapha

Laura clocks out of work for the day. She's not especially passionate about her job as an admin assistant, but at least she gets to work with nice people and doesn't have to take home work after-hours or on weekends. But, this weekend, she might not mind the extra work—at least then she'd have plans. All of her friends are busy or out of town, and without them available, she has trouble deciding what to do. Admittedly, she feels a little lost. She loves spending time with her loved ones and supporting them in any way she can, but she wonders if all the interest she takes in their lives has caused her to lose some of her own identity and distracted her from finding her own true passion in life.

Laura is a vata-kapha—a unique dosha, not because it's rare to find, but because it comprises opposing elements and qualities: Its primary elements of air and earth have attributes that are at exact opposite ends of continuum; what balances vata (air) aggravates kapha (earth), and vice versa. For this reason, it's challenging to predict and describe a typical vata-kapha; if we were to put several vata-kaphas in a lineup, there might be few commonalities among them. What *will* be relatively consistent is their friendliness, contentment, and desire to be supportive. They can effortlessly strike up a conversation with nearly anyone, commonly making friends with strangers on airplanes or while waiting in lines. They find joy in helping others shine in work and life, and they're well-suited for the roles of sidekick or companion. The vata-kapha lacks fire in their constitution, meaning they aren't necessarily leaders or self-starters, so you'll usually find them in the company of others. They like to keep things simple; they want to have fun; and their go-with-the-flow attitude makes them great to be around.

With their mix of opposing elements and minimal fire, vata-kapha's physical traits are less categorical. Somewhere along the spectrum between the lightness of ether and the heaviness of earth, they could be tall or short, sturdy or slight, or have small features or big ones; they are least likely to have average-size traits. As we are more susceptible to imbalances in the systems our dosha governs, the presence of ether, air, water, and earth causes many vulnerabilities for vata-kaphas, such as in their nervous system, joints, respiratory system, and immune system. In fact, their health can seem very delicate, as trying to heal one symptom can swiftly swing the pendulum too far in the other direction. For example, other doshas can heal an imbalance of air or dry and cold symptoms by adding more earth or oil and heat to their diet and routine. It isn't this simple with vata-kaphas because they already have an abundance of earth. Adding too much, sometimes even one drop of oil, can tip the scale. So, staying in optimal health can be confusing to vata-kaphas. They might find that something is working for them, such as a diet or workout, but if they don't make minor adjustments to account for daily disruptions—like having to work late, eating food that's more convenient than it is healthy, or sleeping poorly one night—they may suddenly feel unwell and have trouble understanding why. Some of their more common physical conditions are joint swelling and pain, recurring sinus infections, vacillating between feeling emotionally energized and emotionally drained, and variable digestion. With their contrasting elements, their symptoms and their points of origin can be as varying as their physical attributes, making them difficult to categorize by a single quality or element.

Behaviorally, this dosha struggles with losing themselves in others. As they get more involved in the goals of their friends, family, or coworkers, they often lose sight of their own. With four elements playing a major role in their constitution, they can be well-rounded and have many interests, yet without the fire element to give them determination, they may feel like they never know their own life's purpose or even their identity. Their emotional sensitivity can also be an issue. Comparable to their physical nature, small factors can cause big imbalances; one moment, they can be laughing along with you, and the next they can become greatly offended, even by comments made in the spirit of fun.

Light and Shadow

Vata-kapha's light shines through their selfless support of others, an unparalleled strength. Though we see other doshas come to the aid of others, such as pitta-kapha offering acts of kindness to those they love, vata-kapha's entire world is outside of themselves. They genuinely love to see others succeed and celebrate their wins. They would never try to take credit or ownership of others' achievements, but they feel uplifted and energized by others' good news as if it were their own. As an extension of this strength, they're also likely to be on board with any of their friends' plans and ideas. If you ever need a friend to try a new restaurant with you for the first time, go to a class with you, or offer you moral support by attending a lecture you're giving, vata-kaphas are the ones to ask.

With this flexibility, vata-kaphas struggle to maintain their own identity. *Note: Vatas are shapeshifters when it comes to adapting to their environment, but they're more versed in embracing their identity than the vata-kapha. With only two elements, vatas have an easier time knowing what they like and who they are than vata-kaphas, who are made of four elements.* Vata-kaphas are mergers: When they get lost in supporting friends, their identity merges with others. When they let others take the lead, go along with others' decisions, and put others first, they lose their sense of self, only to discover this when they are without their partner or have time for themselves and realize they don't have any interests of their own. For example, if a vata-kapha dates a sports enthusiast, they might start watching hockey or going to football games. They might keep up on the scores because they know it will be a topic of discussion with their mate. When the relationship ends, they might be left realizing that they never liked sports in the first place; it was just a means to support their partner. It's also true that vata-kaphas may take on others' problems as if they are their own, such as being worried about a friend's lack of satisfaction at work when the vata-kaphas themselves aren't happy with their own job.

The vata-kapha is on this planet to have a good time and to be sure that you're having one, too. Joy is in the driver's seat of their life—while they remain in the passenger seat. The kapha in them makes them take their responsibilities seriously, but their vata characteristics mean that they want to keep obligations to a minimum—so there's as much room for new experiences, connection, and fun as possible.

Since so much of what brings them pleasure involves the company of others, this dosha carries the fear of not having a place in the world or in others' lives. The fun they seek is stripped from them when they don't have someone to share adventures with, and their successes and accomplishments mean so much less when they don't have a companion with whom to celebrate.

My morning routine consists of an early walk with a stop by a local coffee shop. After having many chats and encounters with the barista who worked the morning shift, I made an assumption that her dosha was vata-kapha. This was based on her communication style, her personality and physical traits, and the information about her interests and life outside of work that she had shared with me. One day, she told me that she was a fan of the crowdfunding site Kickstarter, because she loves to see others succeed. I had to chuckle, as she was speaking directly from the vata-kapha script. When I explained this to her, she also laughed. She told me that her passion for being a barista is directly tied to being able to support others. Many times she'll get to know her customers so well that they feel like family, and when one of them graduates from medical school, gets engaged, or lands a new job, it warms her heart to see their happiness and success.

BALANCING VATA-KAPHA

When do you feel most like yourself and most comfortable in your own skin? Do you feel more like yourself when you are alone or with others? Can you voice your opinions and desires with confidence, or do you struggle to understand what you really want?

Communication

The vata-kapha is a merger in so many ways, and how they communicate and interact with others is no exception. They are always happy to chat, participate in (even initiate) a conversation, and they're eager to get to know all about you and your life. Yet, while they'll freely share any fact about themselves, they may be more reserved when it comes to sharing their opinion. This goes hand in hand with having very little fire in their constitution (it's the fiery people that are most opinionated) and an abundance of elements that are quite contrasting (moving between air and earth can cause as much variability in one's stance on issues as it does in their physical traits). Instead, they're more likely to reflect your opinion back to you. Whether you're excited about a trip you just booked, up in arms about a current political trend, or tired at the end of your workday, the vata-kapha will empathize and agree. And this tendency to blend with you isn't limited to the topic you're discussing or the emotions you convey; it can be with speaking style, too. If you speak slowly and with compassion or fast and upbeat, you'll receive the same from them in return. So once again, we find the vata-kapha with ether, air, water, and earth to have diversity within them and with their ways. Perhaps the only qualities we are less likely to see in vata-kapha communication and interaction are the sharp, assertive, fiery qualities expressed by pitta-predominant doshas. This doesn't mean their communication will be void of details or organization—it simply won't be the outstanding attribute.

Stress

Vata-kaphas respond to stress by means of freeze and flight, both of which reflect a lack of desire to deal with the issue at hand. While they will acknowledge they are stressed and readily admit a problem exists, it's more appealing for them to ask someone else to manage their problems for them or to blame someone else for any issues they may have. Vata-kaphas know that experiencing stress is a part of life, but they have difficulty facing it on their own. Stress is disorienting to them, as they don't have the inner fire (pitta) that others use as a guiding light. Everyone should have someone they can rely on in tough times, but the only way for vata-kaphas to get through them is if they're led out of the woods by someone else.

Aside from life's major stressors, the vata-kapha dosha experiences the most stress when they're alone—with no one to guide them and no one to help. Similarly, it's stressful for them to learn that the friends they have prioritized have been taking advantage of their willingness to help or be available. So much of their world is built around other people's lives that they can go into a tailspin when they're left to make their own decisions or don't have plans with others. Though learning how to find their way on their own could be the ultimate way to reduce stress, having time with their friends and family is what will make them feel best.

INSIDE THE VATA-KAPHA MIND

It's easy for me to go with the flow.

I'm generally happy and content.

Though it's easy for me to laugh at myself, as I don't mind being teased or want to cause offense, I also have things I'm very sensitive about.

It seems like the health imbalances I have are usually more sudden, obscure, or harder to resolve than those of others.

Though I'm okay being on my own, I really do prefer to be with others. I might even tend to be codependent.

I prefer for others to make the decisions. I'd rather be the support staff than in a leadership role.

I prioritize others' health and happiness over my own.

Sometimes I feel like my willingness to help others is taken for granted. Every now and then, I'd like for it to be reciprocated because it gives me a sense of belonging.

I can get along with pretty much anyone.

Celebrating others' successes is one of my favorite things to do.

THE DOSHAS OF THE SEASONS

Doshas help us know ourselves inside and out, but we can also give a doshic assignment to nearly anything to give us a better understanding of how various things impact our lives, such as the seasons. Each season has its own distinct elemental makeup and qualities, and therefore, a dosha it resembles most. Summer is hot like pitta, fall and early-to-mid winter are dry and cold like vata, and late winter to spring is wet and heavy like kapha. When we take the season and the "like increases like" principle (page 33) into account, we realize different times of year can aggravate certain people more than others, and that there are imbalances we are more likely to experience as nature changes. Summer will increase the fire element and put pittas at a higher risk of imbalance, creating a potential for more frustration, criticism, and anger. Fall and early-to mid winter increase the air element and cause vata to increase, bringing anxiety, fear, and worry along with it. And late winter to early spring cause water and earth to rise, leaving kaphas more vulnerable to imbalance and an increased likelihood for feeling depressed, sad, and unmotivated.

CHAPTER 9

Tridosha

TRIDOSHA = ETHER + AIR + FIRE + WATER + EARTH

proficient in all trades, well-rounded, a unicorn
(See pages 234 for helpful tables summarizing
tridosha's characteristics.)

An equal manifestation of all three doshas, all five elements, and all twenty attributes, the tridoshic person has our most complete doshic combination. With such a balanced makeup, it can be difficult to describe them in a specific way, as it seems everything fits and nothing fits all at the same time. You will see a mix of all the elements in their physical attributes, and the same goes for their mind and emotions.

The way a tridoshic person presents themselves is a case of nurture versus nature. The strengths and skills that were fostered in their childhood will stand out as they become adults. This certainly doesn't mean they won't discover new interests or talents as they grow older; it merely means that their childhood is the greatest influence on their predominant behaviors and mental tendencies. For example, if their parents are musicians and they live in a house full of instruments with band practice in the garage every Tuesday night, the tridoshic child might have their creative vata dosha nurtured most. Or if they are presented with an opportunity to play sports, they are likely to enjoy participating and could very well end up being a star athlete, having their competitive pitta highlighted. And if they aren't given an option to participate in extracurricular activities but instead go home after school to read alone before helping their mom or dad prepare dinner, their caring kapha side will show through.

This isn't necessarily true of other constitutions. Take kaphas, for example. They may like to participate in a specific sport, but they generally don't love to be active or competitive. If they lose interest but are pushed by their parents or guardians to continue (usually for the sake of being involved or getting physical activity, which they tend to need more of), they may grow imbalanced because they'll be encouraged to go against the grain of what they naturally like or dislike.

In some ways, the tridoshic person is least likely to experience imbalance because they have all qualities equally present. For example, they are equally oily as they are dry. Given this, they are less susceptible to dry skin if they overindulge in drying foods or consume too little oil, and the same is true for the opposite situation, in which they get too much oil and too little dryness. This would be very different for a single dosha; the airy vata would be fine consuming more oil since it balances their dryness, but excess oil would be too much fuel for pitta's fire and too heavy for the watery and earthy kapha. For these reasons, tridoshic individuals don't usually experience a lot of illness unless they grew up in an exceptionally unhealthy environment or have experienced some type of trauma (which takes us back to the nurture versus nature argument).

Yet with all things Ayurveda, nothing is absolute—even the health of a tridoshic person. Should they ever become imbalanced, the process of healing is much more tedious for the same reason they're likely to stay well. Picture this: The tridoshic person accumulates enough heat to experience an inflammatory skin condition. They try to balance the excess heat by adding cool, but because they are both inherently hot *and* cold, there is little margin of error before they overcorrect, swinging to the opposite direction and experiencing a condition of excess cold. So just as easily as we conclude tridoshic individuals are well-rounded and healthy, we could view them as a pendulum that has trouble finding the center once it's in motion.

THE TRIDOSHIC UNICORN

We all see ourselves in every one of the five doshas, since all of them are within us. Yet at the same time, feeling like you can relate to each dosha leads many of us to believe that we are tridoshic. That's simply not the case. While it is indeed possible that you could have all the doshas equally present in you, being tridoshic is incredibly rare. Still, if you believe your constitution to be tridoshic, I suggest that you remain open to the idea of being single or dual doshic. If tridosha still resonates most after you've read through the rest of this book, give yourself a year to observe your shifts and how they relate to nature. A Tridoshic Unicorn will feel balanced in all seasons, where other doshas can feel their foundation rattled in the season that matches their dosha (vata: fall and early winter; kapha: late winter and spring; pitta: summer). For something more immediate, go a step further and consult with an Ayurvedic practitioner just to be sure.

Because this combination isn't very common and can be difficult to describe in any specific physical or mental context, you'll find our discussion on the tridoshic constitution to be very limited here and in the upcoming chapters. Each upcoming chapter on work, love, and family contains a special box dedicated to the Tridoshic Unicorn to show you how this mythical creature might appear. Alas, if you are tridoshic, know that you're not being shortchanged when it comes to self-discovery and learning about your constitution. Just as all the doshas apply to you, so do all of their strengths and struggles, motivations and fears, communications and interactions, and so forth. Every doshic description is relevant to you.

It's very rare for me to feel unwell, but when I get sick, it's hard for me to recover.

I have many passions and pursuits that span across various fields of interest. Learning new things and mastering them comes naturally to me.

I have a lot of acquaintances and close friends. I get along with many people and connect easily and deeply with most.

Though I do have fluctuations in my mood, I can't really identify a trend or pattern with them.

Changing gears is easy for me. I'm adaptable, and I settle in and feel content without much effort.

It's of equal interest for me to have areas of my life where I can be a leader and other areas where I can be supportive and let others take control.

I can act and work quickly when necessary, but I also have stamina and like taking my time.

Making decisions doesn't feel stressful to me, but I don't always need to be the one who decides.

I'll always feel a sense of my own identity, but I can also relate to others quite easily.

I wouldn't describe anything about me as extreme—not my physical characteristics, mood, mind, or emotions.

PART 3

The Doshas in the World

CHAPTER 10

Doshas in Life

Your age changes, but your inherent dosha will always remain the same. Still, it might not feel that way when you reflect on your life. Chances are you've gone through a lot of different phases, some where the person you were before doesn't at all seem like the person you are today. Yet, no matter how many phases you've gone through or different lives you've lived, there's one constant: You have always been, and will always be, the way you are. The unique recipe of elements and qualities you came into the world with will never change. Our mental and emotional traits are an extension of our dosha, so while our experiences throughout the stages of our lives shape who we are, our dosha lays the groundwork for how we will react and respond to those experiences.

While we won't make a shift from being a vata to a kapha, or a pitta to a vata, at any point in our lives, there are some valid reasons why you may feel that this is the case. First, it's possible that you are either currently in a state of imbalance or you were imbalanced throughout your youth (see pages 33–38 for a refresher on imbalances). It's easy to mistake your dosha for your imbalance or to define yourself by how you feel in this very moment, especially if the imbalance is chronic. But moments pass, and if you don't look at the constants in how you act or feel, even if they're buried deep down inside, you're likely identifying your imbalance instead of your dosha. If you feel a strong contrast between how you are now versus how you were in your youth, ask yourself which version of you feels healthiest and most authentic. This will most likely point to your true constitution.

Second, some of your most defining qualities or skills may not have been fully realized or developed until you were an adult. Just as your bones, muscles, and brain were still developing in your childhood, so were many of your finest mental and emotional traits. And everyone and every dosha develops at their own rate—there are early and late bloomers, but there is no dosha that is better than another. Kaphas are usually the slowest to develop, vatas may be more self-conscious about sharing their authentic self, and pittas may feel they need to put on their brave face and only choose to embrace their strong qualities. Still, since so many variables can impact our trajectory, the only thing that is certain is that our talent is always within; it simply hasn't blossomed yet.

Third, you may have learned to hide some of your vulnerabilities and manage some of your less-than-healthy habits in adulthood. Maybe you were shamed or teased about your personality, interests, or trademark qualities and felt it necessary to keep them tucked away. Maybe you liked to dance and twirl in the aisles of the grocery store and your mom would tell you to keep still, or you liked to make your friends laugh but were constantly getting in trouble for talking during class. Perhaps you saw things about yourself you didn't like, such as procrastinating or having difficulty maintaining boundaries, and put in the necessary work to make a change. It can be tough to imagine those emotions or behaviors are still a part of you as an adult, but the truth is they'll always be there.

Stages of life take on doshic qualities, too. From birth to death, there are three major "seasons" that affect your body and mind according to that season's dosha: kapha (birth to puberty) to pitta (puberty to menopause or andropause—the hormonal shifts that happen in early and late adulthood) to vata (menopause or andropause to death). Your inherent doshic qualities are constant, no matter what stage of life you're in, but the relationship of doshas to seasons of life are still important to note. They could be the reason you perceived yourself differently as a child, a factor in fluctuating health, or even what helps (or helped) you maintain balance.

For example, the kapha stage of life will bring out the kaphic qualities in all of us. The emphasis on water and earth during childhood means we all sleep a little more and are a little softer, with a little extra body fat. A kapha during this stage of life is in their season, which could mean all of their innate attributes are enhanced, but it might also mean that it's easier for them to get imbalanced: they may want to sleep *all* the time or be prone to more sadness. When we hit adolescence, we are entering the pitta time of life. It's no coincidence that teens are typically fierier— more rebellious and argumentative—but those who have pitta in their constitution are going to feel these characteristics enhanced until they reach the hormonal changes in late adulthood—perhaps with intense, cystic acne (a kind of inflammation), heavier menstrual cycles, or a more driven and ambitious career life. And after the hormonal shifts, during the vata stage of life, we are all a little more fragile and delicate, like the ether and air elements. If you're a vata, you'll feel this more acutely, with higher chance of breaking or fracturing bones, falling, or losing your memory.

One way to examine how the stages of life might reveal your dosha is through family dynamics, since our interactions with people as we age can point to differences in doshas. Your past is a part of your story, and looking back is like accessing your personal archives, which are chock-full of data on your mental, emotional, and behavioral patterns. They allow you to determine how your experiences may have nurtured you in or inhibited you from growing comfortable with who you are. Having this information fresh in your mind as you read this chapter will help you create more certainty around your own dosha and shed light on ways you can make positive changes that will not only impact your own life, but your family's life, too. So, whether you're reading this chapter with the hopes of gaining a better understanding of yourself or a loved one, take time to consider the following:

1. Were you a healthy child, and was your childhood stable and healthy overall? Were you sick often, or do you feel like you grew up in a state of flux or imbalance? If you felt healthy as a child and grew up in a mostly stable environment, there's less risk of mistaking your childhood imbalances as your dosha. However, if there was less stability in your health and/or your environment, you may have spent much of your childhood out of balance. When you reflect on your childhood and its association to your dosha, you might find it doesn't sync (refer to pages 33–38 to jog your memory on imbalances and the corresponding chart in the appendix to learn about your dosha's tendencies toward imbalance).

2. Did your childhood experiences foster your natural strengths, and were your vulnerabilities recognized and accepted? Were your interests, skills, and values nurtured or were you strongly encouraged to participate in activities you

didn't enjoy or engage with people to whom you couldn't relate? Sometimes kids have internal or external pressures to fit a mold, and this inhibits their inherent qualities from shining through. This is important to recognize in yourself, in part to understand how your childhood impacted your ability to embrace your dosha, but also to move forward and be able to tap into a life that is more genuinely yours (more on that in chapter 13).

3. Think about your strongest childhood memories. Did they imprint positively or negatively on you? Are there imbalances or beliefs you experienced in childhood that you carried with you into adulthood? Are you living your adult life as your true self or a person you were parented and conditioned to be? If you've been living as a version of yourself that isn't true to you, it's likely that your own assessment of your dosha could be rooted in falsehoods.

As we tour through the ways different doshas experience the stages of life and family dynamics, we'll look at the characteristics that are highlighted throughout childhood and adulthood. We'll also explore the influence our dosha has on the roles we play in the world as students and role models, as well as in our own families as children, siblings, and parents.

Vata

Vatas as Children and Students

Vatas come into this world marching to the beat of their own drum. They are individualistic, eccentric, and uninhibited, even if that means they don't fit in with the popular crowd. They are ethereal and airy, energetic and active, and the many mental fluctuations of their mind are often reflected in their physical body. Tapping a pen, bouncing a leg, or playing with their hair, a vata child is often repeatedly told to sit still. Vata children have the slightest frames, the smallest appetites, and the most delicate immune systems. Their constitution can be fragile inside and out, making it more difficult for them to endure physical or emotional stress and leaving them more susceptible to physical and emotional pain and injury.

In home or family life, it may seem like a constant struggle to get a vata child to listen and get their chores done—like cleaning their messy room or finishing their homework. This isn't out of defiance; vatas aren't able to be attentive long enough to complete the task at hand, especially if there are too many tempting opportunities or shiny objects to distract them. It's possible that many children who are diagnosed with ADHD have a stronger representation of vata in their dosha (or could be suffering from a vata imbalance). This also goes hand in hand with their difficulty surrounding routine and schedules. They resist because they like to do what feels best to them in the moment, which is always changing and unpredictable. You can't ask a vata child what they want for dinner in the morning, because they actually won't know how they feel until it's time to eat (and, even then, they'll have trouble deciding). Being disciplined enough to stick to a routine, having more familiar experiences than new ones, and connecting with people whom they find comforting is essential for their physical and mental health and for them to thrive doing the things they love. Finding a way for them to nurture their creative side and explore different interests will allow them to have a fun and happy childhood, but it's important for them to also stay tethered. Without this, they can start to feel anxious, alone, and disconnected.

With regard to education, vatas are fast learners when they are able to focus, but their speediness can be a detriment. Their strength is in their short-term memory, meaning they're likely to cram for tests. They'll memorize their notes the night before, then as soon as the test is through, they'll brain-dump the information.

Vata doshas use their speed to race through tasks, largely because of their limited attention span. Where a pitta may see being the first to finish as winning, vatas simply want to be able to move on to the next activity before disinterest and boredom set in. In the classroom, the vata student is likely to get called out for talking during class or for not staying on task. It's easy for them to get overstimulated, and they naturally discharge this emotion by talking or moving. This relieves the feeling of wanting to crawl out of their skin, a sensation that can arise when they're forced into structure and stillness for too long. Unfortunately, their need to move, fidget, or talk can be mistaken for hyperactivity or an attention disorder, but it's most often a manifestation of their unharnessed creative and imaginative mind. (ADHD is reflective of a vata imbalance. Any dosha can have a vata imbalance, but those who have more vata in their inherent constitution are especially susceptible).

Vatas as Adults, Role Models, and Parents

Vatas won't lose their restlessness as they get older, but age and experience may help them focus their attention and aim their

> ### BALANCING VATA
>
> Who or what (environment, objects, activities, routine) helped to give you a sense of stability and security in your childhood? How might you reach for these tools now for yourself or in support of family members who seem adrift?

arrow, most often toward creative pursuits and unconventional lifestyles. As adults, they're still motivated to do and see as many things as possible, but if they can incorporate grounding practices, they'll be able to home in on their craft, achieve their personal goals, and feel balanced in mind and body. It's only when they're without their anchors that we'll find them spinning their wheels and looking for direction. This puts them at greater risk of imbalances, such as increased anxiety, inability to focus, insomnia, memory loss, and physical symptoms like dryness, constipation, and muscle atrophy. This is particularly true as they enter into the vata stage of life (at the onset of menopause or andropause). In older age, we all naturally embody more of the ether and air elements, but if you came into the world with a predominance of them, your wisdom years might have more forgetfulness, falls, or achy arthritic joints.

Aside from continuing to manage vulnerabilities that were revealed in childhood, the vata adult has to be conscious of how their personal struggles can spill into other life roles where structure is preferred or necessary, like being a parent. We look to our parents for security and leadership, but vata parents can easily lean into a state of anxiety and fear. Parenting in this state can be paralyzing for both the parent and their child; if the parent is indecisive and insecure, the child will lack direction or stability. Taking healthy precautions with little ones is a generally safe bet, but projecting too much fear of the world or new experiences onto the child can limit their learning (especially if they, too, are vata!). And if the vata parent isn't grounded, they may lack some of the self-discipline necessary to enforce rules and boundaries, quite possibly falling into friendship mode or behaving more like the child themselves. In contrast, the vata parent who is confident and comfortable in their skin and has the creativity along with the grounding practices that help contain and balance it will not only influence their children to be the same, but they'll also create a fun childhood experience. They'll raise their kids to be expressive, full of life, and unafraid to step off the beaten path.

WHEN PARENTS AND CHILDREN HAVE OPPOSING DOSHAS

All doshas can find a way to have harmonious relationships, but when it comes to family ties, challenges between doshas may arise. Though there are specific factors at play with regard to your parents' doshas and yours, it isn't genetic math (one pitta parent plus one vata parent will not guarantee a vata-pitta child.) This means that you might end up with a child who has very different interests and needs than your own. If you aren't in tune with this, it can feel like your child has a force field surrounding them that repels your every parenting approach, leading to lots of misunderstandings and broken rules. Vata parents can have difficulty maintaining structure, which can aggravate the pitta and kapha children who like planning, organization, and routine. Pitta parents, on the other hand, revere structure and may push children of all doshas too hard to maintain it; vata children will struggle to meet their expectations, and kapha children will appreciate the routine but won't like the discomfort of feeling obligated to do something. Finally, kapha parents will be the caring softie everyone loves, but that doesn't bode well for vata or kapha children who need more rules, form, and guidance to stay on track. Meanwhile, softness is a perfect balance for the pitta child, assuming they don't see an opportunity for a swift uprising and take charge.

I was an adventurous child, but I also had my share of fears and anxieties.

In school, I had difficulty focusing and sitting still in class. Recess, PE, and art were the exceptions.

I look to my siblings for guidance and support when it comes to family matters. Among us, I'm the one who's a little more scattered.

As a parent or guardian, I find it tough to enforce rules and structure because I have difficulty with these things myself.

Adulting is hard!

Pitta

Pittas as Children and Students

The pitta child, sometimes portrayed as the golden child, is the most self-sufficient of the doshas. Even from a very young age, pittas have an internal meter for goals, accomplishments, and perfection. As they strive to be the best they can, sometimes in a way that is competitive with themselves or others, they are respectful of the rules and structure implemented by parents, teachers, and coaches. They tend to shine in all they do, a sentiment that's true even when the endeavor isn't necessarily of particular interest to them. That's because their main interest is giving everything their all and going the extra mile, no matter if it's home, school, or extracurricular activity. Their rooms are typically organized and clean—perhaps their toys or clothes are evenly spaced or intentionally placed, their homework is done without much fuss, and they show up for practices and lessons on time and with enthusiasm.

But don't be fooled. While their desire to be their best is authentic, their behavior isn't golden all the time. The fire is strong in these kids, which means potential for temper tantrums and rebellion. They can get angry, act out, and quickly lose their cool with anyone, but those in closest proximity to them and most likely to forgive or forget, such as family members, are likely to take the hit. They might unleash their inner dragon on loved ones, but that's usually because they're frustrated with or being too hard on themselves—if things don't go their way, they lose, or they don't think they are good enough.

Pitta's natural habitat is the classroom. They are lifelong learners, whether it's through formal education, self-study, or pursuing relationships that are intellectually intriguing. They value grades and their performance in extracurricular activities, so they make for attentive and exceptional students. In fact, the infamous "my child is an honor roll student" bumper sticker could easily be swapped out for a "my child is a pitta" decal. But because pittas can master things quickly, things go awry once they are no longer challenged. Ever-higher tasks, goals, and objectives are the guiding light of their passion and focus. Without them, pitta's inner fire can be unpredictable, often directed where it isn't welcomed, such as toward classmates or authority figures.

In the same vein, if a pitta child sees any reason to question authority—an overbearing parent or a teacher or coach who is insecure or meek—it could result in a revolt and a complete disregard for people and rules. Just like that, the model student morphs into the troublemaker. This can be a much more common scenario once a child hits puberty, too. While society says it's raging hormones, Ayurveda says it's an escalation of fire, making teenagers more irritable, defiant, and harder to reason with.

In the family dynamic, pittas are the leaders. They are the kids left in charge when mom or dad will be home late from work, who set the (high) bar their siblings are trying to live up to (often resulting in resentment at the kids' table). This is independent of birth order and purely connected to their inherent ability to take on responsibilities with confidence and gusto. But even though they thrive in this role, it's important to be careful with how often the parent fosters it. Praising the pitta child for taking on more responsibilities (of any variety) can reinforce the notion that it's their duty to be everything to everyone and that productivity and success are not simply valued—they're equivalent to love. This leaves them trying to achieve the impossible, forming patterns and habits that will cause them to self-destruct later in life. You might assume all kids know what fun is instinctively, but the pitta child has to learn to make space for play and see it as important and useful as productivity (or learn how much value there is in being unproductive!), and also has to experience failure.

Any dosha can emerge from childhood with a convoluted idea of their worth, but pittas are predisposed to believing that their work, accomplishments, and successes will make them worthy of others' time, company, and love. Because much of what they inherently value matches what is revered in our society, such as money, status, and achievements, it's essential to model to these children how good it can feel to be free from structure and to accept what's ordinary. Childhood can either mold pittas to have both a drive and an appreciation for family, friends, and leisure, or it can shape them into successful individuals who prioritize their

BALANCING PITTA

How were perfectionism and accomplishments rewarded in your childhood? Does perfectionism show up in how you parent or interact with your family? What could a family model that embraces more leisure, fun, and growth made from mistakes look like?

career above all. The pitta who grows up to respect play as much as they do work is a fortunate one, and so are those who get to be in their company. Striking a balance between knowing when to direct attention to responsibilities and when to kick back and relax is a difficult feat.

Pittas as Adults, Role Models, and Parents

It's our hope that pittas move into adulthood with their signature confidence, leadership skills, and zeal, along with an understanding that they will be loved no matter their level of success. Pittas feel at home in the working world; at work, just like in school, they are eager to excel and maintain their achiever mindset. As they enter a stage of life when everyone is building their career, they need to be on high alert for burnout. Pittas are already equipped with a strong fire, and the drive, grit, and determination that's needed to either be an entrepreneur or climb the corporate ladder builds that internal heat—which can cause them fatigue, brain fog, or an inability to function at their peak. So when pittas push themselves to the brink, seeking perfection and optimal results in all they do, they risk not having the energy to enjoy the fruits of their labor, which can breed additional anger, frustration, and resentment.

Not only do pittas have the built-in skill set to thrive in work life, they also have all the tools needed to be the CEO of a family. Their competitiveness comes into play here: They aren't just going to have a family; they are going to have the *best* family. They slide into the role of parents or guardians with ease, as they are comfortable making decisions and being in charge. Still, there's no such thing as being the perfect parent they strive to be. In fact, they may project their perfectionism onto their children in an unhealthy way, setting standards that are typically unrealistic and out of reach—a nightmare for their less focused vata or more relaxed kapha children and inflammatory for the pitta child who has the fire to strive for these expectations but will never meet them. They may also make every effort possible to prevent their children from failures and keep them from making the same mistakes they made (not out of vata fear, but out of pitta perfection), all without realizing that failures and mistakes are necessary for personal growth. With this, pittas become prone to being a helicopter parent by overparenting and limiting their child's opportunities for becoming self-sufficient.

INSIDE THE PITTA MIND

I was the child who liked to have a tidy and organized room.

As a student, I was focused and determined. Getting an education and doing my best was very important to me.

The job of parenting is as natural to me as other leadership roles, yet I have to keep my rules and restrictions in check. I can be too rigid and controlling at times, even though it's an honest effort to keep my kids from making bad decisions or not meeting their potential.

When I was a child, I would become angry if I didn't get my way. Nothing's really changed since becoming an adult, except it's easier to get my way now.

My family looks to me as the responsible one. When someone needs a hand or extra care, they know that I'll step up to help no matter how much is on my plate.

Kapha

Kaphas as Children and Students

The earthy kapha is the poster child for contentment. From the time they're pudgy babies until they graduate high school, they are laid-back and low maintenance, making parenting these children smooth sailing. Due to their kapha stage of life, all babies show more kapha characteristics, with plump features and a vitality that makes us love to hold and be near them. In general, people love to be around kaphas, as they carry a happy and lovable energy. Teachers, parents, and classmates alike get along well with these kids, but because kaphas are most invested in having deep and meaningful relationships, they choose to have only one or two close friends or spend much of their time alone. Slumber parties and extracurriculars may not be their thing, but reading all day or hanging out with adults could be.

Kapha kids love to sleep, but they tend to dislike physical activity and have difficulty getting motivated. This can spell trouble when it comes to weight gain, as this dosha is naturally built with the biggest structure to begin with. In fact, your biggest pushback and disagreements with kapha kids might be related to exercise and drive. They become motivated by things that interest them, but otherwise, they prefer to stay inside and be inactive, putting forth a lackadaisical effort toward things they don't find comfortable or rewarding.

Kapha children don't need to worry too much about illnesses. The kapha dosha governs the immune system, so while wet and drooly kids are top-notch germ spreaders, the kapha child either avoids sicknesses that get passed around school or they have fewer and less severe cases.

At school, the kapha child is relatively low-key. They're typically slower learners, not because they lack intelligence, but because some of the speed and sharpness (air and fire) of vata and pitta are missing from their constitution. They are conflict averse, so it's unlikely for them to cause a ruckus in class or on the playground, and it's uncommon for them to dispute any classroom rules. They don't speak up much, not because they are shy or introverted but because they prefer to keep to themselves. Some teachers may breathe a sigh of relief to have such a contented student who doesn't create challenges, but care must be taken so that the kapha student's peacefulness doesn't morph into passivity.

Kaphas certainly don't want to be the center of attention, but it's still important that their needs and feelings aren't overlooked, especially if they find themselves in unsafe situations, such as being bullied. With their bigger build, slower learning style, and preference for being alone, they can become an easy target for teasing. Because they don't want to cause problems, they aren't likely to stand up for themselves or report these interactions. Thus, it's essential that these students find a way to participate and have their voice heard for the sake of their learning experience and to be sure they don't overly internalize emotions.

The cliché of the homebody might actually be code for the kapha dosha. They are very family-oriented and love a good game night, special dinner, or family outing. Their parents and siblings typically appreciate their go-with-the-flow attitude, but they can also take it for granted. Since kaphas keep their emotions to themselves, they are often seen as the neutral party in any situation and they can be called in to actively mediate family arguments or defuse them merely by being present. Like the responsible pitta, the caring kapha child might need to act as the parent or adult sometimes. Suffice it to say, this isn't their role and putting them in the role of parent or mediator is like punishing them for their neutral attitude. It's important for kaphas to learn how to healthily express their emotions and opinions in childhood—of course, without being forced or pushed to do so—otherwise they may end up watching their life from the sidelines.

Kaphas as Adults, Role Models, and Parents

It's in kapha's nature to avoid change, so many of this constitution's characteristic strengths and struggles in childhood stick with them into adulthood. They can be nostalgic without living in the past, but it's nonetheless accurate to call a kapha "set in their ways." They like to do things the same way they did when they were growing up—stay with the same circle of friends, live in the same city, and tell the same stories. This isn't boring to them; it's comforting. And it also doesn't mean that they don't explore new things; they merely do them at their own pace. They typically feel fulfilled, as the earth is full of grounding elements. Their happiness is something to be envied by the other doshas, who are constantly trying to feed their cravings to seek and learn.

The ultimate nurturers, kaphas are naturals at parenting with affection, praise, and reward. They're like rocks with a soft exterior, so they're proficient at creating a safe and stable environment at home. Because kaphas like to keep the peace, however, they might stall at enforcing structure, guidance, or discipline. And even

BALANCING KAPHA

How have you coped with the changes that come along with being in different phases of life, such as starting or changing a career, moving homes, or getting married? What are the ways you draw a distinct line between being nostalgic and longing for the past so that you can simultaneously appreciate where you've been and be excited about where you're going?

if they don't delay, their sugarcoated delivery will make the discipline seem negotiable.

Even though they can acknowledge that rules exist to benefit their child, what they want most is to see the child happy. As a result, bedtimes may start to get later, homework can start to slip, and unhealthy snacks become commonplace. Perhaps your house becomes the neighborhood hangout, as kids are more likely to get away with things on your watch. Having fun is essential, but such an abundance of compassion without discernment can make a parent more like a doormat or friend rather than the authority they need to be.

INSIDE THE KAPHA MIND

Though I was often encouraged to be more social, I was very content being alone or hanging out with the adults who were around. I could generally get lost in a book or another activity for hours.

As a student, getting good grades wasn't a big priority for me, though I still very willingly complied with teachers and did what was asked of me.

I consider myself a nurturer and I love to see others happy. Thus, as a parent or guardian, I'm challenged by saying no to my child or doing things that would upset them, even when I know it could be a beneficial learning experience for them.

I'm the rock and the peacekeeper among my family and siblings. Because I'm calm, steady, and a good listener, they often come to me when they need a sounding board for their troubles, especially if it involves another sibling.

DOSHAS AND GROCERY SHOPPING

 VATA
The vata tends to make quick and frequent trips to the store. They often forget their list or get distracted and wind up not buying everything they needed, only to remember what they forgot mid-recipe.

 PITTA
Pittas will strategically plan their grocery shopping day, bring a list and stick to it, and insist on bagging their own groceries because they want it done "the right way."

 KAPHA
The kapha person leisurely moves through the store. They'll bring a list, but they'll likely add to it while they shop, especially if they spot an indulgent treat.

 VATA-PITTA
This dosha usually brings a list, but they may still forget an item that was on it. They will second-guess which checkout line is the fastest and might switch lanes once or twice if their line is moving slowly.

 PITTA-KAPHA
Pitta-kaphas will arrive at the store with their list, though they might pick up an extra item if it's on sale or as a special treat for their kids or loved ones. They help people in the aisles and dutifully wait in the checkout line they initially chose, even if it turns out to be the slowest one.

 VATA-KAPHA
Whether the vata-kapha arrives at the grocery store with or without a list, they will often leave with more than they intended. They might make a few trips a week, either to grab something their loved one needs last minute or to get ingredients for a fun recipe they'd like to try. Every time they shop, they make conversation (or friends) with the cashier and other people in the checkout lines.

Vata-Pitta

Vata-Pittas as Children and Students

Eager but uncertain may be the fastest way to describe the vata-pitta child. They have many reasons to be confident and bold, such as their sharp intellect, their quick learning abilities, and their creative problem-solving skills, yet this dosha can be one of the least confident as children. This arises out of their pattern to overthink things. The vata dosha dives into a situation for the sake of experience, not at all concerned about, or aware of, the outcome. The pitta dosha is also on board to take the leap but is sure of themselves and doesn't worry about what others think. The vata-pitta questions everything. While others are having fun and easily letting go of embarrassing moments and missteps, the vata-pitta replays them, comparing themselves to others. They then become self-conscious of doing so, only perpetuating the cycle.

In part out of respect, but mainly for fear of the consequences, you'll find the vata-pitta child to be quite the rule follower. They will take calculated risks, but don't want to do anything that reflects poorly on their character or would cause a need to earn back someone's trust. In their effort to be accepted, vata-pittas are prone to giving in to peer pressure. They can feel it's against their natural instinct (even at a young age it will cause

> ### BALANCING VATA-PITTA
>
> When growing up, do you feel you followed your heart or did you act or make decisions so that you would be accepted, validated by others, or to prove yourself, including choosing a career path based on your family's expectations? List three decisions you recently made where your well-being was the main consideration rather than being accepted by your family.

a visceral reaction), but they haven't had enough life experience to know fitting in isn't always favorable, so they do it anyway.

In the classroom, vata-pittas look for opportunities to fit in and meet others' expectations. They may earn the title of teacher's pet, which isn't necessarily intentional, but being on the teacher's good side makes them feel validated and safe. Vata-pittas find it important to turn their schoolwork in on time and to be at or near the top of their class. They are quick learners like vatas and intellectual like pittas, but good grades don't always come easily. As such they put a lot of pressure on themselves and work especially hard to get good grades, an attempt to both build their own confidence and security and to make their family proud. This can cause this dosha to suffer from severe test anxiety, making it difficult to focus during exams and easy to second-guess their answers.

In family life, the vata-pitta child is the do-gooder, always trying to be on their best behavior to avoid getting in trouble. Their parents know them as the child that does their chores with little to no push-back, but their siblings might know them as a tattletale. They like to have the approval of their parents, and if that means telling on their sister for sneaking out after curfew or hanging out with a crowd she's not supposed to, the vata-pitta will do it. Of course, vata-pittas would love the approval of their siblings, too, but they value fairness and the validation they get from their parents more, so ratting out a sibling (which can earn them points with their parents) is relatively easy for them to do.

Though there are positive benefits to following the rules and striving for fairness, a vata-pitta child that doesn't have any experience in bending or breaking the rules throughout their childhood may see some negative impacts from this virtue as they begin to transition to adulthood—they may fear making mistakes or breaking rules so much that they never question authority enough to develop their own belief system. Childhood is a pivotal time for learning from mistakes and understanding it can be healthy to question authority, as the stakes and consequences from getting into trouble in childhood are typically less severe, and it's when many of our core values develop. A vata-pitta child that is too afraid of challenging something may inadvertently limit the development of their own ideas and beliefs.

Vata-Pittas as Adults, Role Models, and Parents

Vata-pittas are excited to move into adulthood and the world of new opportunities and experiences in front of them. They have dreams and ideas that they want to pursue, and graduating and moving out of their parents' house feels like a fresh start. They can be anyone they want to be, so long as they are willing to follow their own heart rather than their family's expectations. Still, if they haven't yet outgrown the need to be validated by success or others' approval, they could find themselves aiming to please their parents or trying to follow the steps society has determined are worthy: graduate college, find a job, get married, buy a house, have a child. Now or never, the vata-pitta has to debunk the idea that their happiness is tied to their accomplishments or what society says should make them happy and embrace the notion that their greatest fulfillment in life is on the path they choose for themselves.

In the role of parent or guardian, this dosha actively integrates things they valued in their own upbringing and current stage of life into their kids' lives. At the same time, they'll trust the experts over their own experiences when determining what's best. If they hear that a glass of milk is good for growing kids, they'll want them to drink it, even if they themselves don't love milk. The fear and uncertainty we know vata-pittas to carry can be running in the background of each parenting decision they make. Protection and safety always come first. Not a bad motto, but it's essential they don't put their children in Bubble Wrap, because if kids are overprotected, their opportunities will be limited. Understanding the value of their own routine, they'll set up a healthy structure for their family—it would be unlike a vata-pitta to forget to have fun, even if it's scheduled.

INSIDE THE VATA-PITTA MIND

I was an ambitious, go-getter child, but I recall some of that being motivated by a desire to please others.

In school, I had a strong desire to be accepted by my teachers and classmates. I was an exemplary student and somewhat of a teacher's pet.

As a parent or guardian, I find I can parent from a place of my own insecurities. This could show up as being a little over-the-top when it comes to safety precautions or taking extra measures to make sure my child fits in with others.

I'm a blend between the people pleaser and the worrier of my family and among my siblings. In a family setting, I'm often the one asking all the questions to make sure all the boxes are checked—"What time does your flight leave?" "Did you pack your toothbrush?" "Who will be picking you up from the airport?"—or I'm the one who ends up taking on too many things because I can't say no, for fear someone may get upset with me.

Pitta-Kapha

Pitta-Kaphas as Children and Students

Pitta-kapha children seem to be born with their own moral compass. They can be content on their own, finding happiness in learning and exploration in their own way. They'll pick up a book, a chemistry set, or a puzzle and entertain themselves for hours. They are introspective and inquisitive, yet they are often quiet. Rather than the talkative vata or curious pitta child who responds "Why?" to every statement you make, the pitta-kapha asks themselves "Why?"

and seeks out the answer on their own. Despite having a peaceful demeanor on the outside, the pitta-kapha child is a latent rebel on the inside. From a young age, their needs and values are unwavering. When challenged by an overbearing parent or a pesky sibling, they can become stubborn. Aside from these moments of defiance, they are otherwise well-mannered, respectful of authority, calm, and reserved. And, finally, they are accountable. They'll do their homework, practice their clarinet, and step up to take on responsibilities when a parent is ill or not physically or emotionally available.

Pitta-kapha students take a steady approach to learning. It may appear from the outside that they are slow learners, yet in reality, they are methodical and meticulous. They grasp concepts easily, but they also like to sit with information to let it steep, such that they attain mastery over subjects that spark their passion. High marks aren't especially important to them; they are simply a side effect of pitta-kapha's in-depth study. Their reassurance comes from within, not from a test grade.

On the more social side of school, pitta-kaphas get along well with their peers, but their preference is to have a few close friends. At the same time, their lion heart means they'll be the first to stand up to the playground bully for anybody. Seeing the benefit in equality and justice, they have a difficult time standing on the sidelines when someone is being mistreated and will show momentary maturity beyond their years to resolve the problem.

BALANCING PITTA-KAPHA

Have you ever felt yourself taking on extra caregiver roles among your family that are beyond your own children? Create a criteria you could follow when deciding to say yes or no to additional family responsibilities so you can continue to help without sacrificing your own care.

Pitta-Kaphas as Adults, Role Models, and Parents

Pitta-kaphas are internal processors and don't commonly display their emotions outwardly, so nurturing their ability to trust others and express emotion throughout childhood will reflect on how they function as adults. If they keep to themselves as kids and aren't encouraged to talk about their thoughts or feelings, they may adopt a habit of holding things in and accumulating emotions. This dosha, made of fire, water, and earth, will erupt like a volcano when they don't release what's bothering them. When this happens, you'll see their signature patience turn into a trademark temper. Unlike pure pitta, they realize they are responsible for their own feelings and any kind of outburst that may occur. They also have the self-awareness to know that tension rises within if their needs aren't met, like having enough quiet and alone time (and they need a lot of this!). Thus, the stage is set for tempers, outbursts, and holding grudges. Pitta-kaphas trust themselves, but they may find it difficult to let others in. If, in childhood, they aren't presented with the evidence needed to prove that they can feel safe in relationships, it will be hard for them to build lasting friendships or ask for help as adults—and they'll always do their due diligence before feeling they can confide in or depend on you.

THE INTROVERTED AND EXTROVERTED DOSHAS

From the talkative vata to the more reserved pitta-kapha, one could assume that some doshas are more introverted or extroverted than others. It depends on their state of balance, but overall, vatas, vata-pittas, pittas (though internally driven), and vata-kaphas are our more external doshas. They feel energized by interactions with others, enjoy attention from others, look to others for validation, or essentially just express their thoughts or emotions more outwardly.

Pitta-kaphas and kaphas are more internal; they are likely to hold emotions in, spend time alone, find validation from within, and process experiences and problems in their own mind instead of with others. Though these tendencies exist, they should only be one clue in getting to know your dosha. Don't exclude yourself entirely from one dosha because you are introverted or extroverted.

The pitta-kapha parent is adept at creating a stable and supportive environment for their children. They'll recognize each child's unique needs, foster their skills and interests, and gently enforce rules and boundaries, all purely for the children's well-being. Pitta-kaphas are patient and caring, but their way of parenting can have more of a tough-love approach than a pure kapha's would. They aren't known for expressing emotion or giving a lot of verbal praise or reinforcement, so sometimes their love has to be interpreted. While the pitta-kapha parent may need to practice speaking their love outright, especially if their vata or vata-pitta child needs that kind of reinforcement, children of pitta-kaphas can be sure they're loved when they see their parents show up to every soccer game, fix their broken devices, stay up late to help them finish school projects, make them their favorite meal after a hard day, or let them spend extra time with their friends. The pitta-kapha parent is always there when you need them, even if you weren't sure you did.

As a child, I was a lot like the Little Engine That Could. From a young age, I was steady, focused, determined, and calm, unless someone pushed me too hard when I was already trying my best or at a place of discomfort.

When it came to school, doing well was important to me, but I was mainly committed to the subjects I was most interested in. I could happily study those subjects for hours, but everything else felt much less meaningful.

In the role of parent or guardian, I am trustworthy and patient.

Though I give my children adequate guidance, I also give them independence to maneuver through life on their own. Only when they abuse these freedoms or push the limits do I feel my pressure rise.

I often lie low and don't get too involved in family affairs. Still, despite keeping my own thoughts, feelings, and troubles internal, my loved ones know they can count on me to support them in whatever they need.

Vata-Kapha

Vata-Kaphas as Children and Students

The Ayurvedic doshas suggest that our dominant personality traits are a case of nature over nurture, but with vata-kaphas having four of the five elements present in their constitution—and largely the more fluid and malleable ones at that—it is conceivable to think their upbringing may have more of an influence on the attributes that become dominant. This leaves room for debate in how we might describe a vata-kapha child, but one characteristic is certain: Even while young, they value companionship and long to be supportive. Vata-kapha children would rather watch a friend's basketball game from the stands (and treat them to their favorite meal afterward) than participate in the sport themselves. Their involvement in their friends' and family members' lives take precedence over what's happening in their world.

It's wonderful to have a child who encourages others, yet a part of childhood is getting to experiment with different things to find the areas and interests you love. If they miss out on this, vata-kaphas may not really know what career path they want to explore later in life. They may also feel that they don't have a set of values, community, or identity of their own but rather one that's shared with and shaped by everyone else.

As students, vata-kaphas excel when their environment is favorable for them—full of interesting subject matter, with adequate support from teachers and classmates and an emphasis on fun. As long as most of these key components are present, vata-kaphas will find their groove. However, if they start to feel pressure, lack of connection, or indifferent about projects they're assigned, they'll lose momentum. One of the best things a teacher can do for a vata-kapha student is inspire them to find what makes them the happiest so that as they mature, they know how to look for fulfillment within.

> **BALANCING VATA-KAPHA**
>
> Throughout your life, have you intentionally surrounded yourself with like-minded people, or have the people you've spent time with shaped your interests and values? Consider someone from childhood and adulthood who has been a strong influence in your life. How are you similar to them and what qualities separate you?

Vata-Kaphas as Adults, Role Models, and Parents

As long as they're surrounded by happy people and feel that they can support others, vata-kaphas will be able to find joy in all they do. Their job description isn't as important as all the benefits and perks that come along with it. There are numerous reasons why this is well and good, but it can become troubling if they aren't able to craft a career path or begin to imagine what hobbies or interests they'd like to pursue. Remember that this dosha lacks the fire element, which is where drive and passion come from. Given the absence of this element, they're often looking to others for inspiration. This serves them well, but it could become problematic if it causes them to lose their own direction or identity.

As the vata-kapha proudly wears the badge of supporter, many things about being a parent or guardian come naturally to them. They cheer their kids on, are always willing to lend a helping hand, and soak in the success of their offspring. But if we bring it back to the lack of fire in their constitution, we'll see their weak spot: their inability to discipline. It's easy for them to go with the flow, but it can be challenging for them to have structure, to tell a child no, or to hold their ground as a parent. Too easily this constitution can act more like a friend than a parent and in turn, the child ends up running the show. Vata has a similar predisposition, but theirs is out of inability to hold structure; vata-kapha can hold structure and nurture, but they just don't have the fire to lead.

INSIDE THE VATA-KAPHA MIND

Overall, I was a very "go with the flow" kind of child. As long as I had the guidance of a friend, parent, sibling, or teacher, I was content. I would only feel anxious or sad if I were left alone or felt left out.

School gave me a sense of belonging that I enjoyed. In fact, it was the social component that I enjoyed most.

Since I love to support others, parenting is a role I very easily integrated into my life. While caring for children is second nature, it's the structure and discipline that can be difficult for me.

I am my children's, parents', and siblings' best sidekick. I'll go anywhere and do anything with them. I'm available to help and support them whenever they need. At the same time, I don't typically reach out to them in the same way, and I'm okay with that.

THE TRIDOSHIC UNICORN IN LIFE

Tridoshas are adaptable, and having all the elements represented in their constitution means they can be accommodating to all stages of life. As children, they take interest and develop skills in any subject they are exposed to. Though we could say anyone's upbringing is important for development and the path we end up taking later in life, this is especially true for tridoshas. As discussed in chapter 9, nurture has an equal or greater importance than nature in the tridosha's life. Since all things seem to be in their wheelhouse, they'll likely stick with whatever they're immersed in. At the same time, this nurture phenomenon could mean that they aren't given a chance to determine what they're most passionate about, and since their fire exists but could be dimmed by air, water, or earth, they may not have the drive to pursue any existing vision they have.

Just as we saw adaptability in the tridosha's childhood, they make adjustments in their behavior in accordance with their family and the predominant doshas within it. But unlike childhood, this isn't always about what is being nurtured, and the dosha of their children and significant other can require them to make accommodations to what's needed—so long as they are in a state of balance themselves. The tridoshic parent or spouse finds ease in helping to ground the vata, providing calm for a pitta, and uplifting the kapha. And they have no difficulty genuinely sharing interests with their family, because having all the elements as a part of their constitution makes them well-rounded.

CHAPTER 11

Doshas at Work

———

'm convinced there'd be greater job satisfaction, fewer HR complaints, and less employee turnover if we all knew our Ayurvedic doshas and were required to disclose it on our résumés. You've already learned that your inherent constitution tells you so much about how you manage stress, what gives you your drive, and where your potential pitfalls might be hiding. If you apply these characteristics to your career and how you work, it becomes much easier to see the factors that cause obstacles and those that allow you to thrive in your professional life. Using your dosha to enhance your professional life isn't limited to understanding the career paths that best suit you, though knowing your dosha will help with this if you're in need—knowing your dosha also has applications that include what you're like as an employee, coworker, and boss as well as the reasons you seem to mesh well with some people in the workplace while others tend to get under your skin.

We should never rely solely on our dosha (or any personality test) to tell us what we like or what we'd be good at doing, but we can turn to our dosha to help us understand the aspects of a job that will be most fulfilling and where we might find sources of strain. It's crucial to note that any dosha could select any career path and be successful, but one's dosha can strongly influence what broad field of work (e.g., medicine, law, business, education, the arts) they choose in addition to what they specialize in (e.g., cardiologist, family law, marketing director, high school teacher, museum curator). For example, we famously dub vatas as the creative type, but they're not the only ones who will live out creative roles. A creative vata may create abstract, free-form paintings. A creative pitta may be an interior designer who prefers clean lines and symmetry. And a creative kapha might use their hands to make physical objects through ceramics, baking, or woodworking. We're most likely to see vatas in the role of artist, but any dosha can work in an artistic field. Pittas, with their penchant for organization, fill roles as art curators; and kaphas, who love to nurture and watch others shine, study to be art teachers.

The content of the job will clearly relate to your dosha, but we can't ignore the context. We choose work for a number of reasons, and factors like friendly coworkers, flexible hours, salary, the ability to work from home, focus on well-being, or work-life balance may all reflect a particular dosha's needs.

If you're not fully settled on your dosha by now, you'll still benefit from the contents of this chapter. Keep in mind the patterns you've observed in your own professional life, and you may see yourself in some of the examples. Listening to your mind and body as you experience different jobs is important for your *dharma*, or your soul's purpose or intended path. When you are living out your dharma, you are in alignment with your life's mission—which is influenced by your dosha. This alignment can be healing and help to facilitate balance, just as not yet discovering your purpose can make you feel imbalanced.

Your own dosha aside, consider your employees, colleagues, and clients as you read. A better understanding of others will do more than enhance your customer service skills—it could uncover blind spots in how you manage people or projects, lead to better marketing strategies, help you define your company culture, create a healthier workplace, and more. Try using the information you've learned about the doshas to better understand what makes you magnetic to a boss or employee and what could make you repel them.

Finally, if you're confident you know your dosha, you'll get the most from this chapter if you continue to be honest with yourself about what holds you back in your work, where you excel and why, if your career is your passion or was chosen based on external pressures, and how this information could help you fine-tune or redirect your career. Being in the most suitable work environment is as important for maintaining health in body and mind as eating right and exercising.

Let's start with another quiz—well, sort of. How about something more effective than the career path quiz you took as a kid? The following questions and prompts will help you uncover some of your habits, patterns, and strengths in your professional life. Giving thought to these things is yet another way you can relate to your dosha and open your eyes to potential opportunities for growth—clearing the path to a fulfilling career and a healthy life.

1. Visualize your ideal workday. Fill in all the details, such as the hours you work, who your coworkers are, what your work setting is like, even what you wear. Note the ways your dosha's motivations, fears, strengths, and struggles play into a dream day for you.

2. What was (or is) your favorite job? Your least favorite? Comparing the two, decipher what the common denominators are in job fulfillment for you. Take things like the people, pay, schedule, and environment into consideration.

3. Who are the people you love to work and collaborate with? Who do you have difficulty working with? What is their professional relationship to you (colleague, boss, direct report) and does their role impact how well you work together?

Vata

Vata loves creativity, along with freedom and change. Of course, their work must possess these attributes for them to truly experience job satisfaction, so they do well in creative roles, positions that require frequent travel, and jobs that are different day in and day out—and far from monotonous. We find vatas as artists, dancers, fashion designers, travel guides, and keepers of many part-time jobs. This dosha can be quite friendly, outgoing, and talkative, so they flourish when they get to network, entertain clients, or collaborate on projects. On the downside, vatas are likely to have the highest job-turnover rate. The air in their constitution causes them to get antsy and go off in search of the new next-best-thing once their initial job training is over and it's time to get to work. This search for a thrill can happen in any job, even one that has a lot of variety.

Vata employees bring their quickness, adaptability, and love of new experiences to their workplace every day. There's a lightness about this airy dosha that allows them to shrug off disagreements that might cause other doshas to be angry or hold a grudge. While they are great candidates for jobs that require fast thinking, lots of pivoting, and brainstorming new ideas, there can be difficulty when these qualities build up. They can lose focus easily, become disorganized, and have more ideas than they do the attention span and endurance/stamina to implement them. Vatas may also find it tough to get to work on time and meet deadlines because many of the same things that plague them at work are issues at home, like grappling with routine and being easily distracted.

The vata person doesn't often seek to land an executive position, as that would mean sticking to one job or path for a significant amount of time. They find more value in having multiple experiences and would rather not have the pressures and responsibilities that come with running a company or being in a leadership role. Yet, they may climb their way to a leadership position, such as by creating a product that becomes a booming business, even if that isn't what they set out to do. When they get to the top, they'll have a few things to keep in check: mainly their resistance to routine and susceptibility to uncertainty. Vata's tendency to avoid structure can interfere with their ability to give clear direction and their lack of confidence can result in difficulty making decisions. All of these factors can hinder their ability to lead well and feel balanced doing so.

While collaborating with a vata will be an experience filled with creativity and excitement, partnering professionally may prove to be difficult, especially

BALANCING VATA

Think back to a job you quickly moved on from, or a recent project you started but still haven't finished. What prevented you from following through? Going forward, how can you decipher which projects and jobs are truly worth pursuing and what could help you stay more committed and focused on seeing them to fruition?

for certain doshas. The best fit is a pitta-kapha or kapha who will have the patience, direction, and stability to help keep vata on track when their airy nature starts to get the best of them. Pittas and vatas generally aren't a good professional match, as the pitta very quickly becomes aggravated by the spacey qualities of vata—pittas have difficulty understanding why vatas can't stay focused, make decisions, or complete things in a timely manner (an example of vata fanning the flames of pitta). Vatas might like working with each other, finding the other's expansive qualities to be inspiring, but finishing tasks will be difficult with so much air and so little earth or fire. And a vata and vata-kapha connection also has both positive and negative aspects. These two will work together and get along well, but without fire as a component of this partnership, they will need lots of outside direction and motivation to see any project to fruition.

INSIDE THE VATA MIND

Settling on one career path feels restricting.

I need to have a job that is exciting, creative, and feels different day-to-day. Without some or all of these elements, I become bored, have trouble focusing, and get eager to find a new job that feels more fulfilling.

I love working with others. It keeps things lively, plus it can take some of the pressure off me with regard to my responsibilities and performance.

Being promoted, climbing the corporate ladder, and increasing my salary are less important than the experiences I can have in my work.

I don't necessarily aspire to be a boss or manager. Making decisions and leading others isn't my strong suit.

Pitta

Pittas are known for their passion and productivity—and their passion for productivity. It's not fair to label them as workaholics or overachievers, as that sets a negative tone, but by a landslide, the pitta dosha is the dosha most likely to lean in that direction. When they have a goal—and you better believe they have a lot of them—they go after it with fervor. This characteristic is one of the primary reasons we find pittas in executive positions or careers that require higher education. They set their sights high, and they don't let anything get in their way, placing achievements as one of their core values. Second to this, we see pittas in leadership roles or with more authority because they are of the most self-centered dosha. They feel most like themselves when they get to lead or implement their own ideas, and having a sense of control puts them at ease.

Pittas will feel most fulfilled in careers that offer logic, challenge, autonomy, structure, and predictability. They look for positions that will allow for a possibility of advancement (through promotion and continuing education) and seek out the jobs that have monetary reward and high societal status. You'll find them in roles such as doctors,

> ### BALANCING PITTA
>
> Think of a past project, program, or presentation that you put out into the world that didn't go as well as you had hoped. What type of emotion did you experience, and did it match the feedback you received from others? Now, think of an upcoming project you are getting ready to launch. How will your project be received, and how would it feel to be comfortable with any feedback you might receive—potential praise in addition to negative reviews?

lawyers, college professors, CEOs, entrepreneurs, managers, and accountants.

There's a strong probability that your boss is a pitta, or that if you're the head honcho yourself, fire runs in your veins. Pittas feel comfortable in the corner office, and that's great, because they're well-suited for the role. However, even our shiniest qualities can darken the mood if they become too abundant. Being closed off to the input and ideas of others will create a divisive environment and discourage staff and coworkers from contributing. Pittas have a strong opinion on how things should operate—and it's likely based on valid experience or research—but employees want to be heard and could feel undervalued if their pitta boss doesn't carve out time to include them in processes or listen to what they have to say. It's also important for pittas to remember that their passion and confidence, while important for being a good leader, can come across as intimidating. So it's crucial that they stay in touch with their willingness to be vulnerable. Showing their weaknesses or owning up to their mistakes can makes them more relatable. Plus, their staff likes to know they're human.

In the same vein, it's natural for them to have high expectations for themselves, but they have to realize that these expectations may be out of reach for others. Yes, pittas want their employees to do exceptional work, but they need to set standards that everyone can meet. And even though they're too hard on themselves when they think they could have done more or better, it's important for pittas to make sure other people know they appreciate them and give them the recognition they deserve. If they wait to give people praise until they've met (or exceeded) expectations, some of their hardest-working employees will have already applied for and accepted another job before they get the chance.

Since pittas have a lot of drive no matter their professional ranking, this fiery type will likely be the most motivated staff member. Pittas are eager to do their best and prove their worth—even if it's with the vision of ending up in the boss's chair. But when they're willing to achieve this at any cost, it can be a problem. Pitta's hunger for success can make them susceptible to burnout and cause then to mistakenly link their worth with their productivity. So, pittas must be aware of their work habits. They need to know when to stop, when to say no to projects, and when to give themselves the green light for rest and play. Pittas should also be conscious of the difference between being proactive and overstepping their bounds, such as by challenging leadership or having disregard for authority. It's great to speak up and to be invested in ideas and advancement, but even pittas might still have to start at the bottom and work their way up.

When collaborating with coworkers, pittas have to try to stay in their lane. They'll likely be infuriated by vata's disorganization and be impatient with kaphas who take too long to finish projects or speak too slowly in meetings. There's no dosha that can be a match for pitta's attention to detail or their high standards. They work best with vata-pittas or pitta-kaphas, who have enough pitta in their constitution to understand pitta's motives, but not too much fire, which could cause them to challenge pittas' leadership. But no matter the doshas of their staff, pittas have to trust that the structure they bring to the workplace will help keep their team on track without their micromanaging or taking on all the responsibilities. Others will contribute and get to the end product in their own way.

My career is part of my identity. Work often takes priority over other areas of my life.

It's essential that the career path I choose involves challenges and problem solving and that the position I hold incorporates education and has room for promotion and growth.

I can work with others, but I prefer to work on my own. I believe that to get the job done right, you have to do it yourself.

Not only do I want to do my best work, but I also want to be the best in my field.

Being in an executive position or in a role as a leader, manager, or coach feels very comfortable and natural to me. People say I have an entrepreneurial spirit, and I would agree.

DOSHAS AND THE DIGITAL WORLD

Technology, social media, and devices have become a mainstay in our lives. These things aren't expected to go away, but that doesn't mean every dosha approves of, understands, or feels comfortable using them. Here's a glimpse at how doshas have acclimated to living in the digital age:

VATA Devices and social media are good for midday distractions, but vatas don't know how to operate half of the features on their devices because they only have the attention span to learn the things they think they'll use most.

PITTA If technology means evolving and advancing (the two often go hand in hand), then bring it on. Expect them to have the newest model of smartphone and the inside details on the latest apps.

KAPHA

Technology is a part of the changing world, but the changing world isn't the world kaphas live in. Much like the stereotypical old person who can't figure out how to turn on their laptop or upload a file, kapha has an aversion to learning how to use devices and new tech.

VATA-PITTA

The vata-pitta mind is kind of like new tech: quick thinking and there to solve problems. Expect them to pick up technology fast and to be adaptable when integrating new applications but also to doubt their skill level and worry what will happen if the applications crash.

PITTA-KAPHA

They'll adapt to going digital and using devices, just don't force it on them. Be sure to give them time to research which gadget will be the best one and to read the instruction manual to learn all the ins and outs.

VATA-KAPHA

If everyone else is into it, count them in. They'll utilize technology and devices most to keep connected to others.

Kapha

Though kapha people prefer to live with absolute comfort and ease, they are unwavering in their career. With predominant water and earth elements, they'll be dedicated to their work, often staying with a job or company for many years or for their entire professional lifetime. This is partly due to their loyalty to their employer, staff, and clients, but also because they find discomfort in change. Additionally, they often go into a job thinking long-term, as opposed to vatas, who only plan for the short-term, or pittas, who view each job as a rung on the corporate ladder. Their famed nurturing qualities make them attracted to jobs of service; their strong structure makes them good candidates for work that involves manual labor; and with their preference for solitude or small groups, they are drawn to roles with more intimate settings where they develop closeness through interactions—like your favorite receptionist who remembers the names and ages of your kids. For kaphas, a job must allow them to work at their own pace and involve effective direction and leadership. Plus, a good retirement package doesn't hurt. If you know a social worker, teacher, nonprofit employee, or full-time caregiver or parent, they probably have a lot of kapha in their constitution.

> **BALANCING KAPHA**
>
> What areas of your career or work could be more fulfilling if you pushed the limits of your comfort, such as being willing to take risks, raising concerns that might conflict with others' views, or having more uncomfortable conversations? How might stretching your comfort zone be beneficial to you and to others?

Kaphas don't pursue management roles because they desire leadership and achievement like pittas do, but their longevity and devotion to a company may earn them one. They stay with companies through thick and thin, increasing their odds for promotions from tenure alone. If your boss is a kapha, you likely get along well with them, feel your ideas are heard, and don't feel the burden of hierarchy hanging over you when they are around. Even though they're your superior, they still want to be your friend.

While this can make for a pleasant work environment, and one that's conflict-free like kaphas prefer, it could mean you don't receive the constructive feedback and encouragement you need for professional growth. Kaphas like to keep the peace, but at the same time, their friendliness doesn't automatically make them pushovers. Their boundaries are intact, and they can hold their ground when challenged. Perhaps their biggest struggle is accepting change, proving that their boundaries can be good (when they help preserve energy and values) or bad things (when they limit expansion and cause stagnation). Whether it's rebranding, staff turnover, or a move to a new location, they are the least versed in adopting new things.

If the qualities you value most in an employee are reliability and consistency, kaphas are your go-to. Not only will they be steady in the quality of their work, they'll do it while maintaining a kind demeanor. On the surface, this seems ideal, whether you're their coworker or manager. But because they're conflict-averse, you may not know their true feelings about their job. They aren't likely to speak up when there's a problem; rather, they'll stay quiet, withdraw, or avoid interacting with those who remind them of their discomfort. What brings them steadiness can interfere when it comes to adaptability. So, if you're looking for an employee who can easily and frequently pivot—e.g., at a start-up, as a bartender, or in air traffic control—kaphas are last on the list.

For kaphas to work well with coworkers or business partners, their colleague needs to have some lighter and more fiery qualities than they do. If not, the earth that gives kaphas the mental and physical endurance they bring to projects will become heavy, causing the kapha to be the anchor that holds a project back instead of the roots to allow it to grow. Considering this, kaphas make the best collaboration partners with pittas (as long as they don't push too hard!), vata-pittas, and pitta-kaphas.

Though there are aspects of my job that are important, like being reliable and helpful to others, my work isn't the most significant thing in my life.

I want my job to have comfort and security and my work environment to feel relaxed. These are more essential qualities than my job description or the actual work that I do.

Working with others is fun, but I prefer to work with a small group or with people I'm familiar with.

I'm not competitive and I don't specifically set out to be promoted, yet because I am accountable, good at taking direction, and loyal to those I work with, I am often presented with new opportunities.

I can handle leadership roles, but I would really rather not have the added responsibilities or pressure such roles can bring.

Vata-Pitta

A vata-pitta has the intellectual sharpness of pitta combined with the quick action of vata, making them perfect candidates for jobs that allow for innovation, adaptability, and fast solutions. They tend to thrive when they have equal outlets for creativity, evolution, accomplishments, and networking. They're willing to take more professional risks than those who are pitta predominant, but they like more structure, safety, and planning than those who are solely vata. They're also comfy being a public figure, perhaps finding more reward in acknowledgment than salary. Jobs in event planning, marketing, emergency services, and customer relations suit them well.

With strong leadership skills and ingenuity, vata-pittas are more than equipped to be executives, managers, or supervisors in any field. The ether and air elements of vata make them both flexible and moldable, but the pitta gives them the conviction that a sole vata won't have. They bring lots of new ideas to the table and welcome collaboration, as they're not really the type to hold others at arm's length. This is different than pittas, who prefer to do everything on their own. In moments of weakness, they may shift their opinions to match those of their strong-minded colleagues or direct reports, putting some of their authority at risk. Yet their enthusiasm can easily win back the hearts of even their biggest skeptics.

Vata-pittas can present as performers—if not literally (e.g., actors, dancers, and musicians), then in their desire to do well and please others, an extension of their childhood teacher's pet status. But, while a teacher's pet can also be dubbed a Goody Two-Shoes and be unpopular with the rest of the class, the vata-pitta employee is loved. Employers like them for their hustle, and coworkers adore their outgoing and lighthearted personality. The biggest professional difficulty this dual dosha may face is taking on too much in an effort to seek approval from others. Not only do they think that it will reflect poorly on them if they say no, they also feel pressure to make everything they do exceed expectations. Instead of admitting to having too much on their plate, they deplete themselves. They'd rather give the appearance of doing it all with grace than ask for help or quit, as doing so may cause others to see them as weak or a failure or call their skills into question. If you're a vata-pitta, be realistic about doing things for yourself versus others or you could end up on a career path you excel at but that isn't authentic to you.

> ## BALANCING VATA-PITTA
>
> How frequently do you find yourself in a state of overwhelm? Deconstruct what currently has you feeling bogged down and evaluate how you got to this place. How much can be attributed to your desire to do well for others versus yourself? What are three steps you can take to reduce your chance of getting to a place of being overwhelmed in the future?

Like pittas, vata-pittas are comfy in the working world, as they are focused and achievement-driven. This can make working alongside a vata-pitta quite easy, as they'll always get their share of the work done. However, this could be problematic for vata-pitta if they work with someone who is either too slow or easily distracted (such as a vata, vata-kapha, or kapha), as they try to make up for the work their partner isn't getting done, sending them into a state of depletion and burnout. Vata-pittas will find collaborating with pittas and pitta-kaphas (with fire to keep them centered and water and earth to keep them stable) most suitable to them.

INSIDE THE VATA-PITTA MIND

I'm committed to my career, but I have a lot of interests and I'm often tempted to choose another path.

I seek out jobs that have a sense of newness, excitement, and creative problem solving, but I need structure, stability, and certainty to avoid spinning or burning out.

Professional goals are a priority, though, admittedly, I can sometimes prioritize these goals out of a need to meet the others' approval or a fear of letting others down rather than personal fulfillment.

I like working with others, specifically when they can be a source of validation for me.

In theory, I want to be in a leadership role with more responsibilities and direct reports. At the same time, I often second-guess myself and don't always have the confidence or decisiveness it takes to be a leader.

Pitta-Kapha

The pitta-predominant dosha is most focused on goals and productivity, and the vata-pitta dosha has similar focus but with more creativity and greater worth placed on how others view them.

Pitta-kaphas also have great focus and are goal setters, but the added earth element gives them more endurance, makes them more internal, and gives them the interest in and capacity for service-oriented work. If a pitta-kapha is interested in something, they'll give everything they've got to their job. They certainly aren't anti-social, and they're generous when it comes to giving their time and energy to others, but what feeds them most is independent, detailed work (pitta) that comes without the pressure of timelines (kapha). It's also important to them that their work is meaningful and can help to improve the lives of others. Pitta-kaphas are best suited to jobs as writers, teachers, researchers, scientists or lab workers, nurses, or hospitality workers.

Pitta-kaphas are natural leaders, just like pittas. Though they can be sharp and penetrating, the earth element softens their intensity, allowing them to be more patient and interested in the success of the collective. If you report to a pitta-kapha, it might be helpful to know that your boss wants to support you in any way possible, but it's up to you to ask for help. They aren't there to handhold; rather, they will usher you to the resources you need. They want you to succeed, and because they've figured out how to succeed on their own, they will expect the same from you unless you communicate otherwise.

Because of their loyalty, dedication, and ability to stick with things for the long haul to see them to

BALANCING PITTA-KAPHA

What aspects of your work or career are most deserving of your time and energy? Do you have any projects you're hanging on to where letting go or asking for help could afford you more rest and spaciousness? How can you find a better balance between giving to yourself, giving to your work, and your work giving back to you?

completion, pitta-kaphas are very desirable to have as employees and colleagues. You never have to worry about them pulling their weight or packing up and leaving in the middle of the project, and since they are one of the more internal and stable doshas, there's typically never any concern about them getting off task and taking you along with them. Pitta-kaphas work well with pittas, vata-pittas, and other pitta-kaphas because of their shared fire element and goal-oriented qualities. They also enjoy teaming up with vata-kaphas, assuming the vata-kapha can take their direction and won't require micromanaging. And though pitta-kaphas can surely make the most of partnering with a vata, this pairing will be the most challenging for them, since the vata is very external and talkative and the pitta-kapha likes to get buried in their work and keep to themselves.

INSIDE THE PITTA-KAPHA MIND

I'm very dedicated to my career, but I have other interests that will take priority over work, such as time with family and friends.

I find it most fulfilling to have a career that involves deep problem solving and being of service to others in addition to allowing me to collaborate, work independently, and complete tasks at a pace that works for me.

Career advancement is important to me, but it's purely out of the fulfillment I personally feel, not so much for any kind of promotion, reward, or external recognition.

It's enjoyable for me to collaborate with others, especially when it brings together people who are experts in their fields and allows us to share the tasks and rewards.

I'm told I'm a natural leader, but I'd really prefer to just focus on my craft rather than dealing with managing others or with responsibilities that are more related to running a business than my skills.

Vata-Kapha

While work defines many of the other doshas, the vata-kapha is a standout exception. The requirements for their job have very little to do with why they chose it or how satisfied they are with their work. As long as there's harmony, cohesiveness, and time for leisure, the job fits. Still, there are certain career paths that may be better suited for them—jobs that allow them to build relationships, that don't come with a lot of stress or after-hours tasks, and that come with good leadership are ideal. Vata-kaphas make great assistants, front-of-house restaurant workers, massage therapists, customer service representatives, and medical technicians. When you're trying to rebook a flight, asking to switch to a different hotel room, or reporting fraudulent transactions on your credit card, you want their supportive nature on your side.

It would be wrong to say it's impossible, but vata-kaphas don't usually aspire to be in leadership roles and aren't eager to have a lot of direct reports. Should they reach a leadership or management position, it's with the hopes that they'll have a good support staff, as vata-kaphas are timid when it comes to implementing rules and directives. Rather, they are born to play the

> ### BALANCING VATA-KAPHA
>
> What are some components of your work that you feel could be improved, and do you have suggestions for change? Are there aspects or tasks that make you unhappy that you do anyway, simply because someone told you to? List ways that you could stand up for yourself and have your ideas heard. What would be the first step in the process? How do you feel thinking about taking that first step? Can you imagine wading through some conflict or discomfort that eventually leads to greater happiness and fulfillment in your work?

role of support staff themselves, as they are sensitive to others, unlikely to cause disruption or conflict, good at listening and following directions, and able to adapt to a changing environment. Should you have a vata-kapha employee, be sure to check in with them regularly. This lets them know you appreciate them and gives them an opportunity to offer feedback—which they don't tend to do without prompting.

Even without the fire to make them particularly passionate or driven in their work, vata-kaphas can be a dreamy coworker or colleague. They are pleasant to be around, interested in helping, and are good at taking direction (because much of their direction is sourced externally, making them accustomed to looking to others for leadership). In theory, any dosha could work with them, but vata-kaphas should take caution when collaborating with vatas and kaphas, as it can be too much air and earth respectively for them to stay balanced. Vata-kaphas will feel most secure with pittas, vata-pittas, and pitta-kaphas who can comfortably take the lead.

INSIDE THE VATA-KAPHA MIND

When it comes to my job, I prefer to have a position that's fun while I'm at work and that allows me to have fun outside of work. I don't want a job or career that I take home with me.

My career choice is primarily rooted in connection, a sense of belonging, and support of others much more than the field of work I'm in.

Working with others is where I shine, so long as the delegating or decision-making isn't put on my shoulders. I'm good at going along with others' ideas.

While I want to be compensated appropriately for my work, my greatest reward in my professional life is seeing how what I do helps support the success and well-being of others.

Being a part of a support team is much more in my DNA than being a leader. I'll provide help in all ways, but I don't want to be the one in charge.

THE TRIDOSHIC UNICORN AT WORK

It's easy for tridoshas to pick up new skills, since so many jobs
come naturally to them. For this reason a tridosha might feel
aligned with any type of work, but they could also find fulfillment
in careers or positions where there's a little bit of everything—such
as working for a start-up company or building a business from
the ground up themselves. This type of work is more challenging
and overwhelming for other doshas, since single and dual doshas
usually have a few skills that are finely polished. It's also possible
the Tridoshic Unicorn will discover that there's less workplace
drama for them, because, with all the doshas strongly represented
in them, they can relate to and collaborate with other doshas more
effortlessly.

CHAPTER 12

Doshas in Love

There's some truth to the notion of like attracts like: We seek out the same qualities in others that we value in ourselves. In the language of Ayurveda, it might be more appropriate to say that like doshas attract like doshas. Vatas like excitement and are drawn to other vatas, who can make a relationship feel exhilarating. Pittas enjoy organization and planning and naturally feel the allure of other detail-oriented pittas. And kaphas prefer calm and intimacy over adventure, so it's appealing for them to have a kapha partner who appreciates the same.

Like doesn't just attract like, it accumulates like. We are drawn to people and things that are like us, but too much of the same can cause imbalance. But the other half of that maxim, of course, is "opposites balance," which speaks to our common notion of "opposites attract" when it comes to love. Contrasting attributes stop or reverse accumulation, which is why we might feel like someone who is very different from us can make us feel better or more complete. When there are too many shared qualities and not enough complementary ones, one person's unhealthy tendencies will play into the other's, and there won't be enough opposing qualities to establish balance again. In a vata-vata relationship, one person's inability to maintain a routine will eventually destabilize the healthy grounding routines the other has established. Matching two pittas together is akin to pairing up two leaders. When both want to be in control, yet only one can hold the reins, there's bound to be conflict. And in a kapha-kapha partnership, there's risk of stagnancy, as both avoid change and the discomfort that comes along with it. Any pairing with a dual dosha will naturally offer more balance and less risk of accumulation, since it's a union of more elements. If two vata-pittas come together, the sum of the elements is more well-rounded than two vatas or two pittas. If a vata-pitta is coupled with a pitta, there's still a lot of fire in totality, but there is also air to cool (the individuals in the relationship and the relationship itself). And if a vata-pitta and pitta-kapha are in a relationship, they can enjoy their shared interests as pittas, but maintain equilibrium because of the presence of air and earth.

There are many layers when it comes to compatibility in love and relationships among the doshas. Your constitution can influence what initially connects you to a partner, such as personal interests or line of work. But beyond the more superficial things that would deem you a match, your dosha and your partner's dosha will affect how deep and enduring a relationship could or will be. Your dosha determines your communication style, preferred way to give and receive affection, conflict-management style, what you require in a partnership, and what you can contribute to a relationship. All of this can determine how well two people fit.

Any pairing of doshas can result in a healthy, lasting relationship. But this statement doesn't make this chapter null and void—it actually gives it more merit. When you're awake to your and your partner's dosha, you become more aware of your strengths, your vulnerabilities, and what you bring to a relationship. This level of awareness, your and your partner's willingness to put the work into yourselves and the relationship, and your ability to acknowledge and support each other on your own paths will make a relationship work. So, though it's true that certain doshas may find more common ground and make better matches in theory, all relationships have the possibility to flourish if given the appropriate care and attention.

For this chapter to be as valuable and applicable as possible, consider your past and present relationships and what you've learned from each one. This includes relationship patterns in both friendship and romantic partnerships, the greatest joys, and the biggest heartaches. Doing so will enable you to see the link between your dosha and the reasons certain relationships may or may not work for you.

Think both objectively and from a heartfelt place as you use these prompts to reflect. Learning about our dosha is about developing more awareness of yourself and others. What we take away from all of our experiences, whether they're labeled good or bad, is what takes us further down the path of self-discovery.

1. What does it mean to you to be in love? How do you feel when you're in love? The motivations and fears we saw from each dosha in part 2 extend into our relationships. Are there fears that are eased (e.g., being rejected, failing, hurting others) or motivations (e.g., external validation, productivity, change) that are fed by being in a loving relationship?

2. What do you value most in friendships and/or romantic relationships? What are three things that must be present for you to connect with someone? Some of the people we have relationships with will further highlight our strengths, while others pick up the slack, supporting us in the areas of life in which we struggle. Notice how the qualities you value or seek in a relationship are related to your doshic expression.

3. What do you contribute to relationships and what do you look to receive? How do you support others, and how can they be most supportive of you? Knowing your give-and-take in a relationship will provide more clarity as we look toward compatibility between the doshas.

4. Reflect on your biggest heartbreak. What happened to cause the divide, what was lost, and why was that loss so significant? What was your partner's dosha?

Vata

The most adventurous relationship you can have, and also the most dramatic, is with a vata. This creative and spontaneous dosha is sure to bring all the excitement, thrills, and surprises. They love change, are open to trying new things, and are constantly seeking momentum and stimulation in all aspects of their life—and they want to have these experiences with you. When partnered with a vata, you'll travel, attend parties, go to fairs and festivals, make last-minute plans, and adopt the motto of trying anything once.

> **VATA'S DREAM DATE**
>
> Dinner at a new restaurant and spontaneous after-dinner plans like going to a festival, street fair, bowling, comedy show, or karaoke.

Like all doshas, vatas seek the same qualities in a partner or relationship as what they bring. For a relationship with a vata to have any longevity, there must variability, elements of excitement, and action—going to the same restaurants with the same people all the time won't cut it. On some level, they enjoy and even seek drama or major highs and lows in a relationship, like a weekly breakup and makeup. Vatas are so drawn to thrilling relationships that they can confuse them with love. For example, in the initial phases of getting to know someone, they may believe they are experiencing feelings of love; however, it's merely the buzz and excitement that come with meeting someone new. Once these feelings subside, the newness wears off; things become more routine, and vatas are apt to move on, searching for the next connection to make them feel alive in the same way. All the while, the healthiest partner for a vata dosha is one that brings stability, consistency, routine—all attributes that are balancing to vata, the very things they struggle to maintain on their own.

> **BALANCING VATA**
>
> Can you recall a time when you were swept up in the excitement of a relationship only to realize later that you confused the initial thrill with love or overlooked some warning signs because you were having so much fun (or still in the honeymoon phase)?

If you find yourself in a relationship with a vata dosha, know that you are bonding with the light and mobile air element and that you'll be taking on and supporting their active mind, their challenge with structure, and their desire for change. They'll be willing to share and talk about their own feelings, but it may be a struggle for them to listen to yours. This can present an obstacle if conflicts arise in the relationship that need to be discussed, like an inability of the vata partner to plan ahead, remember important dates, arrive on time, or follow through with their commitments. It's also likely that your vata partner will rely on you for planning and organization. Even when they try their hardest, it's difficult for them to stick to a schedule and keep spaces tidy. In fact, if you cohabitate with a vata, you need to develop a tolerance for open cupboard doors, empty bottles in the refrigerator, and dishes left in the sink. These are the call sign of a true vata.

Since the air element causes them to easily and quickly fall in and out of love, vatas usually have the longest list of friends, acquaintances, and romantic relationships—more than any other dosha—and with their uninhibited nature and numerous jobs and hobbies, and penchant to travel, instant connections are bound to transpire. But vatas don't want to settle for singledom, as companionship—even if only temporary—helps them feel secure. Their ideal partners also have a notable presence of vata in their constitution, but they work best with vata-pittas or vata-kaphas who can offer them grounding and direction that they can't find on their own. This allows vatas to have a partner that shares similar interests and needs (all the stimulation, creativity, and change they require to feel whole), yet possess enough of the other elements that it helps to bring balance to both the relationship and the people in it.

INSIDE THE VATA MIND

I love to meet new people.

I've had many romantic relationships and have more acquaintances and friends than anyone else I know.

As much as I'd like to have a lasting relationship, I get restless and struggle with commitment.

Some of the strongest qualities I bring to relationships are my sense of adventure, open mind, and willingness to adapt or change.

I can easily fall in love, especially when there's thrill, excitement, or even drama involved. As soon as the excitement dies down, I start to lose interest.

Pitta

Pittas know what they want in life and they know what they're looking for in a companion, too. As a result, dating a pitta can feel a little like a job interview. They have a discerning nature, which extends to the company they keep, so they want to make sure all the boxes are checked before they let you into their world. But, once they do, you'll be made to feel special and exceptional. A relationship with a pitta will bring passion, depth, and debates. They are very committed partners and strive to have lasting relationships. Though they appreciate companionship, they don't rely on it. They see value in solitude, as they can use the time to focus on their personal growth or career, and they'd much rather fly solo than be in a relationship that isn't adding value to their life or another mark of success. As cringeworthy as the phrases "trophy husband" or "trophy wife" may be, a pitta is most likely to have one.

> **PITTA'S DREAM DATE**
>
> Dinner at a top-rated restaurant or reliable local favorite and an exclusive event (where you can see others and be seen), like a highly anticipated documentary or an invitation-only affair at a museum.

Having a pitta partner provides a sense of security. They prefer to take the lead and make the decisions when it comes to responsibilities, so you'll undoubtedly feel taken care of (unless you're also a pitta, in which case you'll need a serious delegation of chores to avoid conflict). Pitta partners also exude enough confidence to make you confident by association, providing an extra layer to the stability you feel with them. Pittas can be reserved when it comes to verbally expressing their emotions; thus, you'll find their affection shown through what they do, not what they say. If you're receiving gifts, offers to help, and notes from your pitta mate, be reassured that they deeply care for you.

At the same time, if verbal affection is important for you, this dosha may not be your match. Chances are, they won't say "I love you" or compliment your new outfit as often as you'd like, as they prefer direct, essential communication only.

In companionship and when cohabitating, pittas want autonomy and space to lead. For example, a hallmark sign of being in a relationship with a pitta is being told you don't load the dishwasher correctly or catching them reloading it right after you. To their credit, they need this type of control to feel like themselves, as their drive to lead has to be nurtured as much as it needs balance. We'll find this to be especially true if this desire isn't being satisfied in other aspects of their life, such as in their professional life. Still, a relationship will be healthiest for them when their significant other reminds them to soften, break the rules, and be playful.

Pittas will partner best with those who have pitta in their constitution (and will rejoice over an orderly dishwasher), but their significant other shouldn't have the same amount of pitta or the same expression, as two similar firestorms colliding won't end well. In a pitta-pitta connection, someone has to be willing to relinquish control, and that's not always possible. Pittas are better suited for relationships with vata-pittas, who will aim to meet pittas' expectations but will also be willing to let pitta lead, or with pitta-kaphas, who are also happy to support pitta's decisions and follow their guidance. Pittas who are paired with vatas will benefit from

> **BALANCING PITTA**
>
> In friendships and romantic relationships, are you typically the one leading and making the decisions? When does this create harmony and when can it cause conflict? How does it feel to have your partner lead or to experience something in your relationship that's outside of your control?

their playful nature but be frustrated by their inability to make decisions and struggles with organization. Relationships with kaphas will remind them to slow down and be leisurely, a good balance to pitta's productive nature. Yet, pittas may find kaphas to be too relaxed and take issue with them relaxing when there are more productive things they could be doing.

INSIDE THE PITTA MIND

I enjoy meeting people, but I reserve my time and energy for friendships that feel interesting and intellectually stimulating.

I have a moderate number of friends and have had an average number of romantic relationships.

In partnership, I like to have control. This can create conflict, as my significant other can feel like their voice isn't being heard or their wants and needs are being suppressed.

A big way I contribute to relationships is through my ability to care for my partner by taking on responsibilities, being a solid decision-maker, and leading the relationship dance.

Even though I want to be in a relationship, I keep strong boundaries, as I still revere my independence.

DOSHAS AND TV NIGHT

VATA

Has trouble sitting still long enough to make it through a movie or an episode. Watches sporadically and is easily overwhelmed by the endless queue.

PITTA

Favors documentaries, but no matter what the genre of show they choose, they watch while doing something productive (with a tinge of self-shaming and guilt for relaxing).

KAPHA

Can binge-watch with the best of them. Is happy to watch alone or with others.

VATA-PITTA

Tries hard not to watch the next episode without their partner, but because they can't decide on something else to watch, they cave, then try to cover their tracks.

PITTA-KAPHA

Does a bit of research into reviews before dropping into relaxation mode for an episode quite easily.

VATA-KAPHA

Wants to watch with you and for you to choose the show.

Kapha

Your relationship cup will be filled with a kapha partner, as they are affectionate, loyal, and romantic. So much of kapha's personality was built for togetherness: their strength in caring for others, their compassion, and their sweet, supportive nature. They can hold space for your emotional downloads and help rebuild you when you break down. You'll be showered with attention. They bring cohesiveness to the relationship; they never want

> **KAPHA'S DREAM DATE**
>
> Dinner at a quiet neighborhood restaurant or at home before cozying up with a romantic comedy or opting for a puzzle or board game—choosing familiar and quaint activities over new and upbeat ones.

there to be conflict and always want to see you happy. This desire for peace and ease makes relationships with kaphas by far the most resilient—the ones that will stand the test of time.

Kaphas function best when they have deep connection with others, but they're absolutely fine being on their own. Unlike vatas, who look for another person to fill space (kaphas don't like too much stimuli) or provide the earth element they lack, kaphas are stable by themselves. So, for kaphas, being in the presence of others isn't about dependency, it's simply about having company. For example, a kapha usually likes to stay home, either curled up on the couch watching a show or with a book, but they'd rather do it with you (or have you around doing your own thing) than be alone. Their ideal relationship is one that allows them to be alone while being together.

The kapha constitution will be fulfilled in a relationship with a pitta-kapha. They have great compatibility, as both have an appreciation for relaxation, calm, and harmony, but adding some pitta to the mix will assure they never get stuck. A kapha-kapha relationship will also prosper, though the abundance of the immobile earth in this pair puts them at risk for stagnancy. Their least compatible relationship is likely with a vata, as they are destined to have very contrasting interests, values, and habits. Though there's some possibility of air bringing balance to earth, kapha likes to be slow and steady and will feel agitated by vata's fast-moving approach to life. This agitation is less likely to occur if

> **BALANCING KAPHA**
>
> Recall a time where you supported or helped your partner when they were in need. How did they feel, and how did you feel offering your care? Now, think of something with which you could use support but have felt reluctant to ask. How would it feel for your partner to be able to offer support, and how would it feel to you to receive it?

vata is in combination with another dosha, like vata-pitta or vata-kapha, which both have other elements to anchor it and give it structure.

INSIDE THE KAPHA MIND

I have a few close friends whom I've known for a very long time. I've had very few romantic relationships.

I look for deep connections in relationships—quality over quantity.

Sometimes I'm challenged in relationships when there's a need to change or adapt. Because I can be set in my ways, I might be a cause for a relationship becoming stagnant or stuck.

I bring a sense of security to relationships. I'm steady, supportive, and nurturing, and I enjoy caring for my loved ones.

I don't need thrills and excitement in a relationship. I want it to be mellow, easy, and drama-free.

Vata-Pitta

A relationship with a vata-pitta is as adventurous as it is practical, and it's a companionship that emphasizes equal participation and contributions. A blend of the thrill-seeking vata and goal-oriented pitta, vata-pittas like to have time for focus and play; for example, they'll enjoy being settled during the

> **VATA-PITTA'S DREAM DATE**
>
> Reservations at the newest restaurant in town before taking in a concert or other interactive event, like a couple's art class.

workweek with time reserved for social activities on the weekend. You can always count on a vata-pitta to stick to their commitments with you and to show up on time. Known to place high value on others' thoughts and opinions, vata-pittas want to be sure your needs are met, and they also want you to be happy. While these people-pleasing efforts are typically aimed at nurturing the relationship and being accommodating to you, some of it can be self-serving. They'll adjust their schedule to match yours and they'll take on extra responsibilities when they are already overloaded if they know it will win your approval. Others' approval increases their confidence and can be the external validation they so often seek. And their partner's happiness translates to security in the relationship; if their partner is happy, they'll feel grounded in their partnership. And when their giving is met with reciprocity, they'll feel safe and loved.

If there's one thing that will hinder a relationship with a vata-pitta, it's their insecurities. Just as they often question themselves, they can be filled with uncertainty about their relationships. They may constantly worry if they're good enough for their partner, wonder how their partner feels about them, and interpret small comments or actions as signs that something is wrong (like their partner has lost interest in them or taken interest in someone else). They'll ask themselves what their partner could possibly see in them, and they'll frequently ask their partner what they're thinking or how they feel about them. This can threaten the relationship, because the vata-pitta may always feel like they're on shaky ground while the partner tires of having to constantly reassure the vata-pitta that things are in fact stable. This won't be present in all of vata-pitta's relationships,

> **BALANCING VATA-PITTA**
>
> What aspects of yourself do you hold back for fear that sharing your whole self might result in your being rejected? Imagine if you were to share your truest self and be accepted. How would this feel? How would your relationships, romantic and otherwise, change?

since certain doshas are better at offering this reassurance than others, but it will be more of a problem for vata-pittas who are imbalanced or don't have other areas of their life that offer confidence or stability.

The presence of pitta in a companion is ideal for the vata-pitta, as this partner can provide direction and a sense of security that the vata-pitta can often otherwise feel they're lacking. Thus, vata-pittas are most likely to thrive in relationships with pittas, pitta-kaphas, or other vata-pittas. We see less compatibility with vatas, who can cause vata-pittas to feel uprooted, or kaphas, who don't have as much spark or drive as vata-pittas crave. Vata-kaphas can be supportive in times the vata-pitta is feeling less than secure, but if the vata-pitta is looking for a partner to share a hand in the decision-making, the vata-kapha isn't the right mate.

When you're dating a vata-pitta, it's possible they won't want to accept an invitation to go out on a weeknight. That might be breaking too many rules, especially if their to-do list isn't taken care of. However, they'll be up for anything on Friday or Saturday, because the rules say weekdays are for work and the weekends are for going out and having fun. Vata-pittas like to be social and meet new people who have interesting stories to tell.

INSIDE THE VATA-PITTA MIND

I have a lot of friends and acquaintances who span across many different circles and phases of my life.

I've had a moderate number of romantic relationships.

I struggle with continuing to value my own needs in relationships, in part due to my insecurities. Instead, my tendency is to prioritize my partner's needs, with the hopes that they'll like me enough to stay with me.

One of my biggest contributions to a relationship is my willingness and readiness to find equality and compromise.

MASCULINE AND FEMININE ENERGIES AND THE DOSHAS

Within Ayurvedic philosophy is a concept of masculine and feminine energies, an idea that, despite its name, is not connected to gender whatsoever but rather the polarities that exist within us. Masculine energy reflects assertive, active, intense, goal-oriented, and dominant qualities. In this case, "masculine" can be interchangeable with words like *yang*, *solar*, or *heating*. Feminine energy is soft, nurturing, creative, intuitive, and passive. "Feminine" is also referred to as *yin*, *lunar*, or *cooling*. Just as each of us has all of the elements as a part of our makeup, we each have the duality of masculine and feminine within us and our own unique balance of the two energies that we are constantly trying to maintain.

Each of the three doshas has their own balance of masculine and feminine energies, too. Vata and kapha are a stronger representation of the feminine, while pitta appears more masculine. It's important to remember that these are energies that are a part of all of us, and that everyone, binary or nonbinary, has both energies. Anyone, binary or nonbinary, can be any dosha. Because certain ideas about gender have been perpetuated in society (such as that a man is a leader and a woman is a nurturer), without a clear understanding of these energies or the fluidity of gender, one could inaccurately conclude that men inherently have more masculine energy and are more likely to be pitta dosha, and women have more feminine energy and must be vata or kapha. Thus, while these energies are important to consider and embrace, it is essential to separate them from gender.

Pitta-Kapha

If you find yourself in a relationship with a pitta-kapha, you'll be lucky in love. This dosha cultivates some of the most sincere, lasting relationships. They're selective about whom they spend their time and energy with, and once they become interested in you, they become invested. Pitta-kaphas make committed and devoted partners, and they manage to do it without being excessive.

They have their own identity and value their alone time, so the attention they pay you and the support they give will be empowering, not overbearing.

Pitta-kaphas can be quite romantic, and they love to show you that they care through meaningful gestures, such as a handwritten note or a small gift, or with actions, like picking up your laundry from the cleaners or items from the grocery store for you. They'll cook, clean, fix things, or run errands for you without any fuss. Pitta-kaphas give to everyone they love, but this generosity can come at a cost. Friends and romantic partners alike come to expect their dependability and will turn to the pitta-kapha first to be the rock that they need. Concerned they'll create disappointment or send a message that they don't care to those they care about most, the pitta-kapha has a tough time saying no. This can lead to friends and partners taking for granted the pitta-kapha's constant availability and willingness, and then perhaps violating their boundaries.

But the greatest disappointment may come to be their own, should they find themselves having to reach out for a favor. When the strong, unwavering pitta-kapha asks for help but their needs are brushed off by their partner, to whom they have given so much, they will become disheartened. Pitta-kaphas give from a place of genuine and selfless love, but if they feel they aren't appreciated, they will wind up sad and unfulfilled.

Pitta-kaphas are like the O negatives of relationships—a universal pairing that's compatible with most other doshas. A very internal and autonomous dosha, they aren't seeking things from a relationship to feel whole, since they feel quite whole on their own (the result

> ## BALANCING PITTA-KAPHA
>
> How often do you strive to meet the needs of your partner at the expense of your own needs? Could there be a middle path in which you're able to provide for your partner but also have your needs heard and fulfilled? How would you communicate this to your partner and how would it feel?

of all those stable but self-directing elements); they mainly want a partnership that has the same ease and dependability they provide. Pitta-kaphas can make great partners for other pitta-kaphas because of their sincerity and loyalty, yet if one person in this partnership gets stuck, the heaviness of this dual water and earth relationship may cause that person (and the relationship) to have trouble gaining momentum again (this would surely happen in a pairing of pitta-kapha and kapha, too). Pittas also couple well with pitta-kaphas, because the added fire the pitta brings is just the right amount of fuel to give the pitta-kapha the push they need. A partner with more ether and air may be a good fit for pitta-kaphas, who are balanced by the lightness and mobility of these elements, but they'll likely find the pure vata dosha to be too boisterous for them. A vata-pitta or vata-kapha with an upbeat and supportive attitude can feel like a breath of fresh air, so long as they don't bring the instability and restlessness that so often accompany ether and air to the relationship.

Meeting new people is fun and I enjoy being around others, but my preference is to have a smaller circle of friends whom I can trust and connect with in a deep way.

I've had only a few romantic relationships, which have lasted years.

I'm very discerning with the people I choose to spend my time with.

I can struggle with voicing my concerns when there's disharmony or asking for what I need in relationships. I hold it in, and to my detriment and the detriment of my partner, this causes pressure to build until I get angry.

I'm known for bringing loyalty, dedication, and devotion to relationships. Once I'm in, I'm all in.

Vata-Kapha

Vata-kaphas were built for companionship. They find their strengths to be bolstered by the presence of others, and they simply think life is more exciting when there's someone to share it with. Having a partner gives them a sense of security and direction, and they often rely on their relationships to feel complete. Vata-kaphas aren't fond of being alone, so even though they always enjoy spending time with friends, they will become much more dependent on them if they don't have a significant other.

> **VATA-KAPHA'S DREAM DATE**
>
> Dinner at a fun restaurant, followed by people-watching on a park bench, seeing a movie, or sitting in a coffee shop spending quality time with their partner.

Not only does vata-kapha feel most fulfilled when in a relationship, they'll also bring infinite love and support to their companion. Another dosha may feel like they "have" to attend an event with their partner or "should" help them with a project, but the vata-kapha "gets" to do these things and does them with pride and honor. They have very little fire, which for many vata-kaphas means they have very little ego. Thus, they are agreeable and open-minded, more than willing to follow their partner's lead and to try new things. Always ready to talk, vata-kaphas show strength in communicating in a relationship, but this will primarily be listening to their partner or sorting through relationship issues, much less about their own feelings and emotions.

Understanding the comfort vata-kapha has in a relationship makes it easier to see how they struggle, which by no coincidence, is when their partner or friends are unavailable to them (physically, logistically, or emotionally). If their significant other has a big work project that requires them to spend more time at the office, the vata-kapha can start to feel alone and lost without their normal dedicated time together. Should this continue for weeks or months, or be combined with a friend being unavailable for travel or other obligations, the vata-kapha's loneliness and loss of direction will increase. Rather than gaining experience in being alone and learning how to cope, the vata-kapha becomes anxious and depressed, often suffering a loss of identity.

Depending on how you look at it, and depending on your dosha, a relationship with a vata-kapha

> ### BALANCING VATA-KAPHA
>
> Do you feel lost without your significant other, especially when they pursue their own interests and passions? Think of interests, activities, and friendships that you share as a couple and those that are unique to you as an individual. In what ways can you thrive in a relationship while still maintaining your own identity?

could either be easy or a lot of work. For anyone who likes to lead and make the decisions, like the pitta dosha does, vata-kaphas can seem like a great companion. There will never be an argument over who decides what's for dinner or which movie to go to, as the one with the most fire (and opinions) will decide. But this same thing could be a source of frustration if the vata-kapha is partnered with a pitta who doesn't want to have a shadow everywhere they go, or if a vata-kapha is paired with a kapha or another vata-kapha who has the same desire to be the support system instead of the leader. In the case of the latter, no decisions will ever be made. All in all, vata-kaphas need a companion with fire to give them direction and motivation. They will find the best compatibility with a vata-pitta or pitta-kapha, since both of these doshas have the fire that vata-kapha is missing, but not pure fire (pitta), which can feel too intense to the vata-kapha, who prefers to simply go with the flow.

INSIDE THE VATA-KAPHA MIND

I can make friends with anyone. I have a lot of friends and acquaintances, but I also have many friends whom I've known since I was a child.

I had many short-term relationships (lasting for weeks or months) before I found my current partner, whom I've been with for years.

It isn't uncommon for me to struggle with maintaining my own identity in relationships. In everything that I do to support others, I can lose my sense of self.

My biggest contribution to relationships is my undying ability to support, help, and advocate for my partner. While I'm not one to be a natural leader in any relationship, I make the best wingman.

THE TRIDOSHIC UNICORN IN LOVE

The Tridoshic Unicorn isn't the most social or outgoing of the doshas (they end up in the middle of the continuum for most things), yet connecting to others comes easily to them. This dosha is undeniably compatible with all, and with an elemental makeup that affords them not only interpersonal skills but also interests across the board, they're relatively easy to please. The Tridoshic Unicorn's dream date doesn't have to be at a certain place or doing a specific activity; they'll adapt and go along with anything you have planned.

PART 4

The Path Ahead

CHAPTER 13

How to Thrive and Support Others

Until this point, this book has provided you with guidance to help you reach a new level of self-awareness through understanding your dosha. You may need to marinate in that stage a bit, allowing yourself to see how your strengths and vulnerabilities play out in the real world. Try taking the dosha quiz in chapter 2 again, rereading some chapters, or, maybe, sitting on a park bench and people-watching to see what doshas you observe in others. When you're ready to explore some of your newfound opportunities for growth, this section offers goals and actionable points for each doshic combination in work, love, and life. No matter where you are in your dosha journey, there are always ways to thrive!

This section is about thriving and supporting, not fixing or covering anything up. As you've learned, all of us have our strengths and vulnerabilities—our light to our shadow. But it would be fruitless and frustrating to look at attributes that are less desirable as weaknesses that need correcting instead of opportunities for growth and balancing. We need to make sure our shadow side doesn't hinder our ability to function or become a potential source of imbalance; we can do this and still celebrate all of our qualities at the same time.

There are lots of suggestions in this chapter for the way each dosha can thrive in work, love, and life. Rather than tackling them all at once or feeling so overwhelmed that you don't try any at all, consider this approach:

- Begin with the general aspects of your life you feel could use a boost (e.g., day-to-day living, love, or work), but also think about some of the more specific thoughts, feelings, emotions, or behaviors within this area that you find yourself struggling with most or that could use more concentrated attention (e.g., an inability to focus at work, a feeling of not being enough, resentment toward a loved one, or decreased motivation).

- Explore the section on how your dosha can thrive. Select one or two of the suggestions that resonate with you most—those you can see as being workable and effective for your chosen area of focus. If you're not finding a best fit, use the listed items as inspiration to create your own, or read the suggestions for other doshas, since we have pieces of all the doshas in us.

- Determine how you can integrate the suggestions for thriving into your own life. Allow yourself a week to try on these suggestions for size, two weeks of consistent practice with your new perspective and approach, and then reevaluate. It takes time for us to make modifications to our life, and it's important to start small and go slow so that we can stay tuned in to how we feel as we incorporate change. If, after this period, you don't feel like you're on the right track, you can easily make shifts and try new approaches without harm or disruption.

Discovering the intricacies of your mind and learning to offer yourself grace is simply practice for connecting to the people around you, both new acquaintances and old friends. Thus, this process isn't only about becoming proficient in the doshas as they are expressed in you; it's about uncovering the ways doshas are represented in others. Developing this skill makes it easier to perceive the times when your loved ones need extra support and how your superpowers can be useful, or where to seek help from others.

While this chapter can be useful as an all-encompassing tool for interactions you have throughout any given day, it's especially beneficial when you consider the people who play important roles in your life. Take inventory of the different people you connect with regularly. As we saw throughout part 3, some people make good metaphorical dance partners, and others are constantly stepping on your toes (or vice versa). You can't build a world with only your ideal doshas; understanding everyone's unique value—like feeling the joy in all the seasons—will make your relationships better not only with others but also with yourself.

As for supporting others, bear in mind that the idea is to be respectful of their vulnerabilities and to offer grace where needed without causing imbalance in yourself. When it comes to being more sensitive to others and acknowledging where they are on their own path of self-discovery, how can your qualities be of service and where might you be more conscious of checking your shadow side? Offering compassion will only be helpful and healthy when you can maintain your own boundaries and avoid making sacrifices at the expense of your own needs. Being willing to bend is only useful when it doesn't disrupt your own stability and cause you to break. The trick is to look after others in the spirit of genuine support, not just tolerance. Having the energy to support others means staying physically and mentally well and energized; you can't help others thrive if you aren't thriving yourself.

SHOWING UP FOR OTHERS

There are very few things, if any, that we can do without the help of others. Human connection is an essential component of health, and being a part of a relationship, family, or community requires us to show up for others when they need support. What signs do your friends, coworkers, and loved ones show when they are struggling and need help? How do you come to their aid? What type of support do you like to receive from others? Who gives you support and how?

How Vatas Thrive

Create, but Contain

Having the capacity to create and explore is a must for vata, but without the structure to contain it, there's a risk of mental and physical energy becoming so diffuse and scattered that it depletes. So, while creativity is essential and shouldn't be forgone, it can't be without the daily anchors, bookends, and landmarks that ground vata. This could come in the form of a schedule—one that isn't too rigid or constricting: for instance, a schedule surrounding work or professional life that has consistent timing with already-established health and self-care practices. For some, this may be establishing sleep and eating times and sticking to them as much as possible; for others, it may mean committing to consistent morning and evening routines to help give them the conscious feeling of the start and end of a day. Instituting routines can send a message to the body to stay synced with its own natural rhythms.

Schedules are one of the least appealing things to vatas (the word alone can make their whole body contract), but schedules can actually create room for spontaneity, one of the most attractive things to vatas. When they plug the nonnegotiables and absolutes into each day in a reliable way, their free time is clearly outlined. This means fewer decisions have to be made about use of time and there's a lesser chance of experiencing stress from scrambling to get things done last minute (or dealing with the repercussions of not having done them at all!).

Supporting Vata

If you're not a vata, there are ways you can help a vata friend, coworker, or loved one in their process of learning to create, but contain. Go easy on them when they arrive late, miss appointments, or lose track of things. A free pass isn't warranted or required, but understanding that they aren't hardwired for planning and organization is supportive in and of itself. Build a little extra time into your dates with them since you know they have trouble being ready on time. Give them soft and gentle reminders to keep them on track: "I'll see you later tonight." "Looking forward to our appointment tomorrow at ten AM." "I saw your keys on the counter, so you know where they are when you're ready to leave." And finally, try not to overwhelm their busy mind with too many details or decisions or tempt them with excessive options or opportunities.

Look Before You Leap

The most impulsive of the doshas, vatas have to keep their attraction to all things new and different in check. While they do need a constant sense of renewal and change to feel whole, an inability to pause and decipher between what's purely a temptation or distraction and what's worth pursuing can result in unfinished projects, lack of commitment in relationships, and an overall diminished sense of direction in life.

Not getting distracted by every glowing opportunity (shiny object!) may always feel like a work in progress for vatas; nonetheless, it's still important for vatas to practice patience and discretion. One way to do this is by keeping an "ideas journal," since vatas are notorious for dreaming big and often. Writing down thoughts that relate to new projects and ventures can be done daily. They can then be reviewed on a monthly or weekly basis to decide which are worth implementing and which were simply an idea for and in the moment. This can both release some mental chatter and also prevent vata from jumping into something too quickly. Another approach would be to reserve excitement and adventure for specific areas of life. For example, searching for newness or thrills in a career, home, or relationship may not be as healthy as looking for them through other outlets, like painting the kitchen a new color or taking a vacation.

Supporting Vata

To be the voice of support and reason for a vata, you must understand that this need to have change and newness in life makes them feel like themselves. Rather than discouraging it all around, be a sounding board for them. Let them talk through their ideas with you. Ask them questions that help them make the most informed choice and reflect on times in their life when change has been good, but also times when making decisions in the moment have led them astray—discuss whether a change is necessary at all. And as a part of supporting their urge to make changes in a mindful way, also be sure to ask them what they need from you once they do leap into something new. Help them weigh the pros and cons of staying in their current job or taking a new position, but also find out what they will need when they begin working for a different company.

Talk through what ending a ten-year relationship might be like, but inquire how you can be available for them when they do.

Mobilize to Stabilize

Vata's superpower—physical movement—can be an ally in grounding and staying focused, but like the many things that vata needs to stay balanced (like creativity and change), an excess can cause them to feel imbalanced. They key to this superpower is to know how and when to put it into action.

Vata's main cue to move is experiencing an overactive or unsettled mind. And though it isn't always predictable, that familiar antsy feeling is often patterned—perhaps occurring after an attempt to focus for an extended period, after sitting too long, or in midafternoon, when most of us could use a break. So, while vata could just wait for the inability to focus to arise, it makes as much sense (or even more) to get ahead of it with planned movement breaks. And when the time arises, consider the type of movement that would bring balance or be a counter to what's being felt. If vata is experiencing quick and fleeting thoughts, they should try slow and methodical movement like a walk, yoga practice, or qigong. If it's rumination or worry, they can be more literal with grounding themselves; try lifting weights or doing some stretches while seated or lying on the ground or floor.

Supporting Vata

As vata's confidant, you probably won't need to remind them to get movement in, but you may have to encourage them to do the opposite: to slow down and seek comfort in stillness. You can infer that their mind is moving at warp speed through their darting eyes, fast speech, or need to fidget. But asking vatas to stop all movement would be quite jarring to them and could cause more anxiety than calm, so there's no need to command them to sit still or settle down. Instead, respond to their indicators by being a safe and calming presence. Be aware of your own breathing and mannerisms, by slowing your breath and rooting your feet into the ground or floor—focusing on how your feet keep you connected to the stable earth element. It's easy to get caught up in their energy, as it can be uplifting and intoxicating, but with vata, movement begets movement. You'll be of better service to them and yourself if you're able to keep yourself grounded in their whirlwind.

How Pittas Thrive

Soften and Share

Many of pitta's standout qualities, like their mental acuity, leadership skills, and drive, are all in direct alignment with their sharpness. This attribute is necessary to make pittas feel like they're on their game and in their zone, but it can come with an intensity that can be intimidating and off-putting to others. Pitta's sharpness sets a tone of extremes, where there's only room for right and wrong or black-and-white, and it creates a rigidness that can be detrimental to their well-being and those around them. When pittas seek to soften, they'll find it easier to keep their calm and their connection with others.

For pittas, it's helpful to remember there's more than one way; like water, it's possible to be strong and soft. Planning, organization, and being laser-focused on goals can hold pittas captive, and they end up making many sacrifices in the pursuit of perfection. When the search for perfection starts to build, sharpness can accumulate. But if pittas soften through outward expression of emotion and vulnerability— something they may normally view as weak—they can save themselves a lot of heartache. Being willing to be vulnerable, especially in front of others, reminds them that they're human. It helps them keep realistic expectations, prevents them from pushing too hard, and makes them more approachable and relatable.

Supporting Pitta

When you notice a pitta friend, colleague, or loved one becoming as sharp as a razor's edge, you can support them by being a soft landing place for them. Rather than getting pulled into their intensity—trying to keep up with any unrealistic expectations they have for you or contributing to negative dialogue that erupts when they are feeling frustrated—keep your state of calm and let some of your own vulnerabilities show. Share a story about a time you had to ask for help, reveal a mistake you made, or disclose one of your vices or a bad habit you're trying to break. Be willing to let your emotions be seen—both tears of sadness and joy. Opening up to a pitta in this way creates an air of solidarity so that they feel safe to do the same. Showing up in a genuinely attentive and caring way can be exactly what's necessary to sweeten the spicy pitta.

Lead While Listening

Since pittas are so certain of their own abilities and skills, it can be difficult for them to strike a balance between taking the lead and being inclusive of others' ideas, thoughts, and feelings. In many cases, they want things done their way and don't put a lot of trust in others to do things right. On an elemental level, this drive causes fire and heat to build. On a practical level, it isolates them from others, as it's not desirable to be around someone who doesn't put their faith in you. It's not good to strip pittas of their leadership roles, since those roles feed their soul, but pittas can prevent heat from accumulating and stay in good standing if they listen while they lead.

Listening means tuning in to others in addition to cultivating self-awareness. When pittas feel frustrated, angry, or critical toward a boss, employee, partner, or family member, the source is often something that's not going right in their own life. When they're not aware of this, it can be easy to place the blame on someone else, only perpetuating the cycling of distrust. Realizing that they're lashing out because of something personal is a process that requires patience, willingness, and an open mind. Pittas must be able to reflect on their emotions and past interactions in an objective way, noticing when their anger sets a tone that makes it even more challenging to have difficult conversations with a clear mind or accept outcomes that aren't in their favor. When they can see this as a pattern, it makes it easier to recognize when it could happen again, so they can either pause before they speak or remove themselves from the situation entirely to let off some steam. And when pittas pause to take time to listen to themselves, it makes it easier for them to be mentally and emotionally available to others—something that allows everyone to learn and grow. Pitta's employees will feel empowered, their loved ones will feel seen, and pittas themselves will realize it's more sustainable to work with people than against them.

Supporting Pitta

For those who don't identify with the pitta dosha but can see it strongly in a colleague or friend, consider playing into their desire to lead in a way that could result in more trust in you. First and foremost, this comes by knowing and trusting yourself. The more versed you are in your abilities and the better you can communicate your needs, the more comfortable pittas will be with you handling responsibilities of all sizes. Your confidence will go a long way, yet you may find your pitta boss or partner still isn't open to hearing your opinions or suggestions. Pittas are too often so enthusiastic about their own ideas that they fail to consider yours, so you might have to trick them into thinking your good idea actually was theirs. Start by planting the seed, then help them imagine it and connect with it on a personal level. This isn't with the intent of being manipulative and absolutely isn't a suggestion to hand over ownership of your intellectual property, but it can be a good first step to help pittas open up to a new idea (that isn't their own).

Be Productive, Yet Playful

Although they may not see it, pittas are worth more than their diploma or salary and loved for so much more than their successes. While encouraging productivity will help shore up their innate passion and drive, pittas also need to play—but not in the "work hard, play hard" way. Pittas don't have to take things to the extreme; rather, they can manage a to-do list while sprinkling in moments of play, and they can also take a more playful approach to all things productive.

While they won't find balance by adding equal parts work and play, they can find it by taking time either daily or weekly for dedicated "nonproductive" or "goal-free" time. This time is purely for play or things otherwise deemed frivolous. We can expect pittas to gasp and balk at the mere suggestion of this, or if they seem open, they might start planning what to do in their goal-free time. Instead, they should choose to do what feels fun and fulfilling in the moment without plans or expectations—so long as it isn't work.

Supporting Pitta

You can come to a pitta's aid by planning a playdate with them. Try to keep activities free from competition or anything that might tempt them to measure progress—like volunteering for a charity event, going for a walk, visiting an orchard for apple picking, or baking cookies together. Whatever you invite them to do, try to draw their attention to the process and experience rather than the end product. Left to their own devices, they will tie productivity to everything they do. Be aware that they may still find their own way to tie a goal to any activity (like raising the most money, walking the fastest, picking the most apples, or making the cookies identical in size or decorating them in the most perfect way), but with your help, they'll learn to embody the ways leisure and play restore and recharge them. They may possibly even notice more play helps them to reduce stress and be more productive in the end.

How Kaphas Thrive

Routinely Change

While pittas love to have a routine, kaphas *are* routine. Their love for consistency and comfort makes the contents of their days very standard—what would feel monotonous to others can feel heavenly to a kapha. This is well and good, as keeping a routine ensures our days will have form and rhythm, like nature's cycles. But kaphas aren't too eager to change if or when they realize their routine is serving them well. Thus, instead of their routine being a healthy path for them, it becomes a deep groove that draws them into a state of imbalance.

Kaphas can enjoy the comfort and consistency they need to keep their equilibrium and simultaneously shake things up enough to maintain a forward trajectory. This can be done by establishing times for periodic self-check-ins to assess how they're feeling, reaffirm their direction in life, and consider if their routine is contributing all it can to their well-being. Since our needs shift during different seasons and phases of life and predictable change is easier to cope with, these routine changes can be very fitting for the invariable kapha.

Supporting Kapha

Since kaphas especially like to do things on their own time, it's important to be available when they're ready to reach out for help. If you push a kapha, you'll be met with great resistance, often resulting in inaction or the opposite of what you had hoped to achieve. So instead of probing them to take action, look for signs of readiness from them (e.g., prioritizing exercise, researching healthy eating, joining a support group, asking for a recommendation for a therapist). If they don't ask for your help outright, you can ask them the best way to be their supporter or accountability partner. Whether you're yelling from the sidelines or right there with them as their teammate, they won't want to let you down. Making changes to an established routine can be a very personal process, but there is still room for help from a friend.

Give and Receive

Kapha's disposition to be nurturing and caring puts them in prime position to give, but since they're so used to giving and are often less practiced in receiving, they can struggle to accept when their kindness is reciprocated. The heavy earth element provides kaphas with a fullness that other doshas don't have, but even they need to refill their cup. Giving more than they receive can leave them feeling empty and cause them to neglect their own self-care, ultimately diminishing the energy reserves they use to care for themselves and others.

Receiving takes practice. For someone who's used to saying no when help is offered or feels undeserving when gifted with something special, learning to be receptive to smaller things can help. They might consider accepting compliments with confidence or begin a gratitude journal and write down at least one thing they are grateful for each day. And for the loving kapha who wants everyone around them to be happy, they need to remember that people like to help—and being receptive to that help can actually make them feel better.

Supporting Kapha

If you know a kapha who has difficulty receiving, the best thing you can do is continue to give to them—they can't practice receiving without you! Just as they are starting small, do the same by giving them sincere compliments or offering random acts of kindness. Write and send them a letter or a card, bake them cookies, bring them fresh-cut flowers from your yard, or tell them how smart they are or how much you admire their patience. You can also try to reciprocate their giving ways and to be a model recipient when they give to you—making sure to show your gratitude and appreciation for them. This gives them opportunities to receive with grace and as a bonus, you'll build a stronger relationship with them in the process.

Motivate and Circulate

Kapha's inherent slow and static characteristics keep them (and people around them) grounded in our overbusy and overscheduled world, but they lack the fire element that provides the spark to get them moving, and it's much too easy for them to become stagnant. Moreover, they are quite comfortable being stationary, so their inertia begets inertia. Thus, for kaphas it's important to find regular ways to stay motivated and stay in motion for their health and balance.

On the most basic level, exercise is key for kaphas. Moving one's body not only increases physical circulation, but it can also free up stagnation of the mind by allowing time for mental processing. Kaphas like exercise (even though they often have to be tricked into doing it) when they recognize it makes them feel better. So, once they get started and build it into their regular routine, they usually keep up with it. The tough part is getting the ball rolling, and for that, they should start with small, accessible increments—walking a few blocks or stretching for ten minutes, and then increasing from there. The idea of tackling something more can be too daunting and make them decide against it before they've given it a try.

Supporting Kapha

As kapha's companion or confidant, think of yourself as their cheer-leader. Give them a pep talk when they are ready to jump into action and give them applause at every little milestone. Reward them with something that gives them comfort—like a home-cooked meal or a coffee date with them. You can also motivate them by joining them in their endeavors. Accompany them to a fitness class or on a walk, but always let them choose the activity and allow them to set the pace. The last thing you want is to discourage or intimidate them. While you should aim to make up for some of the fire they're missing with stimulation and motivation, remember your job is to encourage, not to tell them what to do.

How Vata-Pittas Thrive

Solve with Stamina

Thriving in emergencies, vata-pittas are quick to act with clarity and effectiveness. They are our go-to people when looking for rapid responses and quick solutions to acute problems. And as much as we rely on them, they also need to be hands-on in these types of situations to flourish and feel whole. But vata-pittas are built for speed, not for endurance, and the mental and physical energy put forth in crises and emergencies is short-lived. Without acknowledging this, they can find themselves in a state of depletion and feel like a strong gust of wind has put their fire out.

Being able to solve with stamina involves pacing and having a vision of what it looks like to see a project through to completion. The sharp and fast vata-pitta loves the excitement of starting something new and can get the same adrenaline rush in the beginning phases of projects as they do in managing emergencies. But not everything is an emergency, so it's essential to have an idea of the required steps, time, and resources it will take to maintain or finish, instead of coming out blazing. It can be useful for vata-pittas to carry a planner to reference when considering adding one more thing to their calendar. This can be especially helpful if appointments and the time needed to allocate to responsibilities are clearly marked or color-coded to offer an accurate visual representation of how busy they already are. And even when this planner is in tow, they can still practice saying "let me check my schedule" before committing. This way, there will be change to contemplate whether or not they have the time and endurance for another book club, work task, committee, fitness program, or friend date—all things we might see a vata-pitta get involved with and then find themselves juggling too many things at once.

Supporting Vata-Pitta

For the vata-pitta in your life who has tenacity but little endurance, think of yourself as the aid stations on a marathon course and them as the runner. They've committed to the race and are going to give it their best, but they may need to stop so you can hand them an electrolyte drink or a Band-Aid. They may not know if or when they're going to need your support, but if you know them well, you might be able to predict what they'll need and when, helping you to place aid stations in all the right spots. Since it's usually work projects or family obligations that overflow their schedule, they're more likely focused on responsibilities than they are on basic needs—which is exactly where you can fill in. Set up a schedule with them for meal or grocery deliveries or combine a friend date with running errands. You should also recognize that as much as they need to take breaks to recharge, it may not be the time to invite them to lunch or a special event, especially knowing that they won't want to miss out and will have difficulty saying no.

Choose Your Own Happiness

Vata-pittas are known to question their worth and turn to external sources as a form of self-validation. They have high expectations for themselves, and they are very conscious of others' opinions and ideas. Self-awareness and awareness of others is a wonderful quality to have, as it can foster personal growth and sensitivity toward others. But when it causes one to question their abilities or to modulate their behavior, especially based on a perception, it can inhibit happiness and become unhealthy. This is a real risk for the vata-pitta, who can lack confidence and look to others for approval.

To combat this tendency, vata-pittas have to do what makes them happy, not what they think should make them happy. They have to believe in themselves from the inside out—to feel internally the external validation they receive. They can do this with a simple self-inquiry before making any decision (accepting a work proposal, saying yes to a date, or even deciding what to wear in the morning) and asking themselves whom they are making the decision for, if the decision is authentic to them, and if their decision will bring them joy. Others already trust in them, but vata-pittas have to learn to trust in themselves.

Supporting Vata-Pitta

To reinforce vata-pitta's decisions to be in alignment with their happiness, be conservative when offering your opinions and always give them space to decide. They put a lot of weight in your thoughts, actions, and words, so even when you're not aware of it, you're likely influencing them in some way. This could be on a small scale, ranging from comments you make about a movie you saw or a book you read, or on a bigger scale, such as how you feel about certain people or a company they are considering working for. They'll want to see the movie you liked and avoid the book you didn't (or read it, but not tell you they did). They'll be hesitant to meet the person you didn't get along with and will accept the job with the company you raved about. They do think for themselves, but because they value you, you may play a bigger role in their decisions than you realize. Keep this in mind and take caution when your vata-pitta friends are making decisions, and instead of adding what you think, ask questions and make statements to prompt them to choose with their own guidance and wisdom.

Stay Grounded in Your Expectations

The vata-pitta dreams big and has every intention of reaching their goals. We all should embrace the notion of the sky being the limit, but we also have to keep our feet on the ground while we stretch toward the stars. Because vata-pitta has very little earth element, this makes it difficult for them to keep the ground within reach. As such, they can set unachievable goals and expectations that are too high for themselves or anyone else to meet.

For vata-pittas to stay grounded in their expectations, they have to be willing to see and accept all outcomes. If they can't envision an outcome other than the ideal one they keep dreaming about, they're likely to be let down. Sitting quietly and working through all possible scenarios and how each makes them feel can help them hope for the best while learning to be comfortable with what's the least ideal (How will they feel if they don't get the promotion they're up for? What will it feel like if their flight is delayed and they miss their best friend's wedding? What emotions could arise if the offer they put in on the house isn't accepted?). In addition, it's vital that they keep an eye on the present and the past—since the future tends to be where their mind lives. Mindfulness practices, specifically breathing exercises, are exceptional tools for keeping one's mind in the moment. A simple, three-minute practice of sitting with eyes closed and inhaling to a count of four, then exhaling to a count of four can be invaluable. Staying in the present will help alleviate anxiety about what's to come, and reflecting on the past can give them insight into what they've already overcome to get to where they are today.

Supporting Vata-Pitta

Under-promise and over-deliver to your vata-pitta friends and family, as it's easy for them to get their hopes up. Their anticipation could purely be a manifestation of their mind, but what they anticipate is very real to them. When making plans with vata-pittas, include details to avoid them filling in gaps with their own imagination. The dinner date you plan with them may be very whimsical and romantic in their mind; meanwhile, you're intending to take them to a local diner where the music is played so loudly you can't have an intimate conversation. Include what a backup plan might look like so they know that there's a chance plans will change and how that might affect them, even if it's what movie you'll see if you can't get tickets to the one you were hoping for. And most important, don't offer to do something you aren't certain you can commit to, even if you're thinking aloud or mentioning an idea in passing. They'll remember that you said you wanted to have coffee with them on the weekend and will clear their schedule so they can meet you. Yes, they still need to do their work in keeping their own expectations realistic, but you also have to do your part. Stick to your word and be clear about your intentions.

How Pitta-Kaphas Thrive

Let It Out

As you might recall, pitta-kaphas land on the internal side of the continuum. They keep their thoughts, emotions, and needs to themselves, which makes them respectful and contemplative beings. However, when they hold everything in for too long instead of voicing their needs or processing things in another way, feelings will accumulate, pressure will rise, and an eruption will ensue. To stay in a state of balance, pitta-kaphas have to let it out.

For someone who isn't used to sharing their inner monologue, journaling is a perfect option and a great first step toward opening the lines of communication with others. This could be a general practice, a dedicated time when you can put thoughts from the day down on paper. Or maybe it's more specific, like writing about a recurring issue with a friend or an emotional event that hasn't seemed to settle. No matter the topic, the experience of processing their emotions through journaling can ultimately make sharing and opening up to others feel more commonplace and natural.

Supporting Pitta-Kaphas

How receptive you are when listening to pitta-kaphas can be a major factor in whether they choose to voice their needs and emotions. Because it takes time for them to build trust, you must be steadfast, but not pushy. Wait for them to bring up their divorce with you instead of asking them to relive it, or simply tell them that you're willing to listen when they're eventually ready to talk about it. Be available to them and give them time to initiate a conversation—no need to pry or probe. When they do finally open up to you, listen without judgment so that they will be encouraged to continue to share. Maintain eye contact, nod your head, and give any verbal or nonverbal feedback to let them know you're paying attention. They're choosing to share with you because they trust you, but they won't continue to share if they feel like you're being dismissive of them.

Stay Focused, but See the Panoramic View

Pitta-kaphas take lots of trips down rabbit holes, researching their work or taking deep dives into personal topics of interest. This is all well and good, until they get tunnel vision or forget to look up from their work long enough to notice what else there is to see. In some ways, this is to be expected, since they have minimal amounts of the expansive elements of ether and air, but being able to focus and see the panoramic view is important for maintaining balance.

Though pitta-kaphas prefer depth, it would be a healthy practice to occasionally participate in something in which they will only scratch the surface, like being a guest at a friend's activity or event—bonus points for not researching it ahead of time. Stepping out of their comfort zone to expand their horizons makes them more adaptable and kindles an enthusiasm for new things. New activities and short-term commitments can balance the pitta-kapha, since they are typically associated with ether and air elements, of which pitta-kaphas have very little. At the same time, having no activities and no commitments can be balancing, too! Pitta-kaphas notoriously get so buried in their work that they're oblivious to signs their body or mind is getting tired. It's too easy for them to burrow through without rest, so it's good for them to take breaks during a workday and a set aside a full weekend to relax.

Supporting Pitta-Kapha

If you know a pitta-kapha who is susceptible to going down the rabbit hole with projects or getting buried in their work, find ways to be the uplifting, energetic source that can pull them out of the zone and make them refocus on their well-being. As their friend, you're at an advantage because you're one of a small, select group that they'll trust and listen to. Ask them how they feel, if they've taken time for self-care, and if their needs are being met. They respect you and will answer in earnest. And while you certainly don't want to push, rush, or force them, if you offer a simple invitation to participate in something with you that will help them decompress or give them a gentle nudge to make more time for themselves, they will likely accept and take action. Respect their need to focus, but encourage them to be expansive and to emphasize their health, too.

Maintain Boundaries without Closing Doors

Pitta-kaphas are some of the most loyal and dedicated people around, but they are also reserved and discerning. So, though these qualities make them great companions, pitta-kaphas can be difficult to get to know. It's authentic for them to take their time and do their research when it comes to something new (they'll do their due diligence with people, too), but it can also seem unwelcoming or cold to those that don't yet understand this about them.

Their gut instincts are strong and most often accurate, yet it's essential for pitta-kaphas to remain open to others and to be aware that these tendencies might make them seem uninterested. While they shouldn't fake it (they probably wouldn't be able to if they tried), they should know how others might interpret their encounters. A way to practice being open and building new relationships, while remaining true to their pitta-kapha self, is a monthly "new friend date." For this designated date, they'll reach out to someone they know and whose company they enjoy as an opportunity to better get to know them. This could be coffee or lunch, or a short event with a predetermined beginning and end to keep commitments minimal while still offering a chance for connection.

Supporting Pitta-Kapha

Pitta-kaphas crave sincere and meaningful conversations, and having this in mind when you interact with them can be a fast track to earning their trust. They take your actions and words at face value, even when they're in jest, and will hold you to your promises. It's unlikely they'll show much interest in talking about the weather, traffic, or other topics that are often used to fill awkward quiet space, but that doesn't mean they aren't interested in you. Be yourself, but remember, pitta-kaphas can take a long time to get to know. Give them time, be persistent and consistent. Knowing this up front will help prevent misunderstandings and make for honest and long-lasting relationships.

How Vata-Kaphas Thrive

Initiate and Ignite

We know vata-kaphas are comfortable in the passenger seat—they'd rather go along for the ride than navigate or drive. Being a companion is their strong suit, in part because their airy and earthy nature allows them to go with the flow, and in part because their fire element is too minimal to spark a desire to lead. But we have to remember that fire isn't absent in them (or anyone) entirely, and recognizing and calling upon their inner flame from time to time is necessary for them to stay balanced.

It's not specifically essential that vata-kaphas be able to lead others so much as it is for them to be able to carve out their own path. One way they can work toward this is to designate one day or night a week to do an activity on their own—bonus points if it's something they've never done before. Taking this initiative will help them discover their own passions while still allowing them room to support others.

Supporting Vata-Kapha

It would be too much pressure for your vata-kapha cohort to make all the decisions, but asking them to narrow down the choices or make a final decision can be just the right thing to ignite their fire. Ask them to tell you the name of a few movies they are interested in seeing, then you can choose which to get tickets to. Or narrow it down to two restaurants for dinner, but have them make the final call on where to make reservations. If even that feels like too much for them, at least be sure you're always asking them for their thoughts, opinions, and perspectives—they may always match yours, but giving them an opportunity to contemplate is important. Finally, make sure they don't take personally any bad experience you might have had when they were guiding the way (the movie they chose wasn't good or the restaurant they picked had terrible service). Should this happen, they'll be discouraged from taking charge and making decisions next time.

Celebrate Yourself

For all the times the vata-kapha shows up for others, it's equally important that they show up for themselves. It fills them up to celebrate others' wins, but recognizing their own milestones is an even better way for them to feel fulfilled. They don't need to celebrate a major accomplishment to do this, but it's important that they allot time for self-compassion and self-love. Making this a weekly occurrence by blocking their schedule for a few hours one morning or evening a week would be ideal, but even once or twice a month would be a good start.

With this, vata-kaphas have the most exciting assignment of all: to show themselves love in their own chosen way. They can buy themselves flowers, take themselves out on a date, take a full day off work for play, or spend time reading in a coffee shop. What they choose may feel indulgent and therapeutic, but it might also be challenging for the vata-kapha who spends very little time focused on themselves.

Supporting Vata-Kapha

Supporting your vata-kapha friends in celebrating themselves is a joyful assignment. Lift them up by honoring what you know is important and significant to them by reflecting their own support, and letting them know that you appreciate all the times they've had your back. They would rather have the attention placed on you instead of them; still, they'll appreciate having you cheer them on and how it feels to be seen. Since they tend to put others first, they may be surprised that you've noticed what's happening in their life, but giving them this care can make them more comfortable being seen by others and ultimately have a lasting impact.

Be Supportive While Standing Your Ground

With a desire to always show up for the people they love, vata-kaphas have a tendency to put their own needs on hold—especially when they feel their perspective or desires might clash with others. But vata-kaphas don't have to choose between themselves and others, between listening and speaking, or between being supportive and standing their ground. They can, and should, do it all.

The way to become proficient in these polarities may best be practiced through embodiment, since vata-kaphas' physical and mental attributes represent elements on opposing ends of continuums. They can literally stand their ground by taking a broad stance, slightly bending their knees and feeling the strength of their legs and the earth beneath them. With their hands over their heart and eyes closed, they can repeat "I am supportive" to themselves as they inhale and "I stand my ground" on their exhale (repeating this mantra five times while holding their stance)—remembering what this feels like in their body. Then, when put in a situation in which there's an opportunity to offer their opinion, they can recall this sensation and feel empowered.

Supporting Vata-Kapha

Be very aware of how easy it can be to take advantage of your vata-kapha friends' willingness to merge with your values, and be cognizant of their boundaries, especially when they have trouble establishing them on their own. It's easy to become self-absorbed around vata-kaphas, as they'll play into your every wish and follow you as you take the lead. Because playing the role of companion is true to their nature, vata-kaphas have difficulty drawing a line between their natural support of you and sacrificing a piece of themselves to maintain the relationship. If your loved one is a vata-kapha, always make sure that their well-being has been considered, that they know their needs and can assure that they are being met, and that their identity is intact and recognized.

How Tridoshas Thrive

Stay in Season

Tridoshas will experience their best health when living in harmony with the seasons. Each season possesses more qualities of one dosha: late winter and spring are kapha, summer is pitta, and fall and early-to-mid winter are vata. In the season of their respective dosha, people have to be more cautious of imbalances as their environment contributes to accumulation (like increases like). Tridoshas have all the seasons happening inside at once, so they have to stay alert to how their environment is making them feel at all times of year.

There are many ways to live in accordance with the seasons: choosing to eat produce that's locally and seasonally available, adjusting exercise to complement the season (e.g., more vigorous in spring, slower and more methodical in fall), or taking time for a reset with specific foods and self-care to restore during the transition between the seasons.

Supporting Tridosha

Honoring the seasons can be a wonderful way to come together with friends or a community, specifically with seasonal traditions. Spring festivals, summer cookouts, fall visits to a pumpkin patch, winter solstice gatherings—there are many possibilities for marking the season and giving certain times of year a recognizable feel while supporting one another's health. If you have a tridosha in your life that you'd like to help maintain balance, start your own seasonal traditions that are unique to your interests and your relationship. Add a new tradition to your calendar now, commit to it annually, and watch the tradition and the connection to your tridoshic loved one evolve.

Use Your Inner Compass to Map Your Way

With all the elements expressed quite evenly, tridoshas tend to relate to many types of people and find connection with nearly every activity they try. This can make finding their own way and passion difficult, as they'll find everything outside of them relatable—nearly everything they do and every person they are with will feel like home. But just because someone is good at something doesn't mean that they were meant to do it, meaning tridoshas might have even more soul searching to do to find their true direction.

To map their way, tridoshas first have to open themselves up to as many experiences as possible. And in doing so, it's important they stay aware of how each experience makes them feel. For example, they might consider how it makes them feel physically, what emotions are brought to the surface, and how easily they are able to find a state of flow. In the end, they must look inside, as all the answers are within.

Supporting Tridosha

You can support your favorite tridosha in mapping their way simply by being in tune to how your actions highlight different parts of their personality. Notice if their interests trend in the same direction as yours and what activities make them the happiest. While they might love cooking with you, joining you for a yoga class, or watching the same genre of movies that you do, help them get to the heart of what truly feeds their soul. Encourage them to try new things and be willing to explore new interests with them, especially if you see them losing their drive or simply going through the motions.

Embrace All Elements

Every dosha has their light and shadow, their strengths and struggles, and what fuels them and what can cause fury. At the core, this is all based on the elements and elemental properties that exist within. While single and dual doshas typically have to perform checks and balances on one or two elements, tridoshas need to embrace them all.

Like incorporating all the flavors and nutrients you might need in a meal and modifying when one gets low or is depleted, tridoshas should evaluate their daily routine to be sure all the elements are represented. For example, the light and mobile ether and air can be brought in through exercise. The water and earth elements can be included by oiling feet at night before bed. And the fire can be tended to by drinking a cup of warm water first thing in the morning. Or on a mental and emotional level, ether and air can be embraced through staying open-minded. Fire can be represented by pursing one's passion. And water and earth can be fulfilled when given proper time for mental rest, such as with meditation.

Supporting Tridosha

As the tridosha strives to embrace all the elements, you can support them by embracing the different moods and emotions that they embody. While having all of the elements means the tridosha can be very well-rounded, it can also mean that they are more complex and less predictable. As their companion, this can make it difficult to anticipate different reactions and imbalances that come with daily stressors in the way that's possible with other doshic combinations. Learning to accept all the components of their personality and being prepared for anything can help the tridosha maintain balance and thrive.

Your Dosha, Your Story

———

The experiences we accumulate throughout our lives write a story, one that's told through the way we think, feel, and behave. In practicing Ayurveda, I've learned that listening to my patients' stories is a critical part of being their guide on a path toward health and healing. Their personal timelines are filled with mental and emotional landmarks, physical symptoms and imbalances, failures and triumphs, all of which provide meaningful insight into their truest nature. These are clues that help me to see my patients for who they really are, at their core and in their wholeness. And, in most cases, they are able to do the same in turn. This establishes a foundation for their lifelong well-being, as feeling seen and seeing one's true self are healing. This brings forth awareness and connectedness, which open space for love and compassion toward ourselves and others, states of being that must exist before we can feel well.

Our dosha gives us a clearer perspective on our strengths and vulnerabilities, what feeds our soul and why, and why we feel so aligned with some people and at odds with others. While we are shaped by life's events, it's our dosha that makes our responses to these events predictable. When we know our dosha, we can forecast the reactions we'll have, the emotions that will surface, and the feelings we'll need to manage.

Our dosha doesn't allow us to predict the future, but it can equip us for the ride ahead, no matter the terrain. It's advantageous to be able to identify thought and behavioral patterns as potential obstacles in our personal lives, careers, and health, but perhaps even more beneficial is knowing what to do when they arise. There's no separation between our mental and physical health, so the good that comes from knowing our dosha doesn't stop at having a better understanding of our mind—it carries over into every part of our well-being. There's a connection between the way we think and the way we feel, just as there is a connection between us and nature (the microcosm and macrocosm). Ayurveda's offerings for self-discovery and healing are boundless, but this can mean it's easy to forget to see ourselves as a part of something bigger. So, as you embark on this journey, stay open to seeing the forest when among the trees and the ways you can live in harmony with yourself and the world.

Dosha Quick-Reference Tables

	ELEMENTS	ATTRIBUTES	PRIMARY ACTION	ASSOCIATED THOUGHTS, FEELINGS, OR BEHAVIORS
VATA	Ether + Air	· Light · Mobile · Subtle · Cold · Dry · Rough · Hard · Clear	Movement	Light: creativity, excitement around change, spontaneous, generating ideas, joy Shadow: fear, feeling scattered, anxiety, depression, grief, ungroundedness, difficulty sleeping, forgetful
PITTA	Fire + Water	· Light · Sharp · Hot · Liquid · Oily (dry in excess)	Transformation	Light: sharp intellect, attention to detail, goal-oriented, well-focused, problem solving, ambitious, self-motivated Shadow: overly ambitious, perfectionist, critical, hostile, aggressive, violent, ego-driven, fails to give praise, may only see what needs fixing
KAPHA	Water + Earth	· Heavy · Oily · Soft · Smooth · Dull · Dense · Cloudy · Gross · Static · Cool	Protection and growth	Light: forgiveness, compassion, stability, nurturing, content, mental endurance, giving, caring Shadow: attached, greedy, difficulty starting new things and accepting change, easily gets stuck in a rut, lethargy, uninspired, depression, neglects self-care, too few boundaries, can be seen as a doormat

Vata

OVERVIEW OF VATA DOSHA		
ELEMENTS	Ether + Air	
ATTRIBUTES	· Light · Mobile · Subtle · Cold	· Dry · Rough · Hard · Clear
PHYSICAL TRAITS	· Small or tall frame · Curly or kinky hair · Dark or black hair · Dry skin · Irregular teeth · Small or thin lips · Small eyes	· Active or darting eyes · Brown or black eyes · Lean or easily builds lean muscles
MENTAL CHARACTERISTICS	· Creative · Spontaneous · Adaptable	· Enjoys change · Joyful · Lighthearted
COMMON IMBALANCES	· Constipation · Irregular digestion · Gas or bloating · Overactive or restless mind · Hyperactivity · Fear · Worry · Insecurity	· Lack of stability or difficulty keeping routine · Insomnia or waking during the night · Fearful dreams · Dry skin · Nerve pain · Osteoarthritis

VATA'S LIGHT AND SHADOW SIDES	
LIGHT	SHADOW
Adaptable and welcomes change	Unable to commit, with excess turnover in personal and professional life
Thrives in beginning phases or when starting new projects	Doesn't always see things through to completion
Full of new ideas	Has trouble focusing on one thing at a time
Creative	May struggle with simple A to B solutions
Spontaneous	Challenged by keeping a stable schedule
Verbalizes emotion	Can have excessive or unnecessary speech
Outgoing	Fears missing out

VATA IN LOVE	
LOVE LANGUAGE	Words (verbal or written), play
RELATIONSHIP STRENGTHS	Openness to change, willingness to talk, ability to be spontaneous, adaptability, adventurous attitude
RELATIONSHIP VULNERABILITIES	Difficulty with commitment, need for lots of support in making decisions, instability, constant search for action and stimulation
QUALITIES THEY VALUE MOST IN RELATIONSHIPS	Adventure, excitement, action, freedom, fun

Pitta

OVERVIEW OF PITTA DOSHA		
ELEMENTS	Fire + Water	
ATTRIBUTES	· Light · Sharp · Hot	· Liquid · Oily (dry in excess)
PHYSICAL TRAITS	· Medium or average frame · Fair or reddish-toned skin · Fine or straight hair · Blond or red hair · Early to gray or bald	· Average-size teeth that may yellow · Average-size eyes · Intense or penetrating eyes · Green or gray eyes · Average muscle mass
MENTAL CHARACTERISTICS	· Natural leader · Detail-oriented · Sharp intellect · Goal-driven · Focused · Self-motivated	· Competitive · Organized · Planner · Responsible · Accountable
COMMON IMBALANCES	· Fast digestion · Loose stool · Blood in stool · Hyperacidity · Ulcers · Anger · Irritability · Judgment · Excessive criticism · Difficulty falling asleep · Violent dreams	· Acne · Rashes · Psoriasis · Inflammatory conditions · Conjunctivitis · Reproductive hormone imbalances · Hypertension · Anemia

PITTA'S LIGHT AND SHADOW SIDES	
LIGHT	**SHADOW**
Self-motivated	Ego-driven
Natural leader	Can be bossy or controlling
Results-driven	Has trouble playing or relaxing, prone to burnout
Critical thinker	May only see what's wrong or needs improvement, fails to give praise
Passionate	Intimidating
Organized, plans well	Rigid
Sharp intellect	Sharp tongue, unfiltered speech

PITTA IN LOVE	
LOVE LANGUAGE	Gifts, taking on responsibilities
RELATIONSHIP STRENGTHS	Confidence, reliability and respect for routines, passion, leadership, strong decision-making and planning skills
RELATIONSHIP VULNERABILITIES	Need for personal space and autonomy, desire for control, excessive structure or rigidity, prioritization of work
QUALITIES THEY VALUE MOST IN RELATIONSHIPS	Intellectual challenge, companions who are equally passionate about careers and personal interests, cleanliness and organization, partners who are goal-oriented, space to lead, autonomy

Kapha

OVERVIEW OF KAPHA DOSHA		
ELEMENTS	Water + Earth	
ATTRIBUTES	· Heavy · Dull · Cool · Soft · Smooth	· Static · Cloudy · Gross · Dense
PHYSICAL TRAITS	· Broader or bigger frame with proportionate weight distribution · Oily skin · Thick hair	· Very dark or very light-colored hair · Strong white teeth · Big eyes with thick lashes · Bulkier muscles and trouble losing weight
MENTAL CHARACTERISTICS	· Compassionate · Loyal · Trustworthy · Nurturing · Grounded · Even-keeled · Serene	· Calm · Kind · Joyful · Good long-term memory · Strong mental endurance
COMMON IMBALANCES	· Slow digestion · Mucus in stool · Depression · Withdrawal · Apathy · Lack of motivation · Feeling stuck · Allergies · Asthma · Respiratory conditions	· Edema or fluid accumulation · Stagnant blood or lymph · Congestion · Diabetes · High cholesterol · Prolonged sleep · Growths or tumors · Fibroids

KAPHA'S LIGHT AND SHADOW SIDES	
LIGHT	SHADOW
Grounded and stable	Gets stuck easily
Natural caregiver or nurturer	Neglects self-care
Compassionate	Too few boundaries, can be used as a doormat
Good mental and physical endurance	Slow-moving
Excels at maintaining what's established	Can be self-limiting when it comes to new experiences
Excellent long-term memory	May be overly nostalgic for the past, can hold grudges
Outgoing	Fears missing out

KAPHA IN LOVE	
LOVE LANGUAGE	Touch, food or cooking, offers of help
RELATIONSHIP STRENGTHS	Unconditional love and support, compassion, help and care, stability
RELATIONSHIP VULNERABILITIES	Getting stuck easily, becoming too comfortable, conflict aversion, accepting problems instead of addressing them
QUALITIES THEY VALUE MOST IN RELATIONSHIPS	Ease, joy, steadiness, stability, commitment

Vata-Pitta

OVERVIEW OF VATA-PITTA DOSHA		
ELEMENTS	Ether + Air + Fire + Water	
ATTRIBUTES	· Light · Dry · Subtle	· Hot or cold · Rough · Hard
PHYSICAL TRAITS	· Small to medium frame · Normal to dry skin · Fine to medium hair · Red or blond or brown hair	· Average-size teeth · Green or blue or brown eyes · Lean to average muscle mass
MENTAL CHARACTERISTICS	· Quick-thinking · Responds fast	· Innovative · Adventurous
COMMON IMBALANCES	· Dry eyes · Red eyes · Rheumatoid arthritis · Hard acne · Melasma · Variable bowel or irritable bowel syndrome	· Hemorrhoids · Endometriosis · Adrenal fatigue · Infertility or difficulty conceiving · Depletion or burnout · Insomnia

| VATA-PITTA'S LIGHT AND SHADOW SIDES ||
LIGHT	SHADOW
Strives for fairness	Becomes resentful easily
Quick to respond	Fatigues and loses motivation quickly
Aware and cautious of others' feelings	Sometimes acts out of fear
Thinks and learns fast	Can make errors or take shortcuts to solutions

VATA-PITTA IN LOVE	
LOVE LANGUAGE	Words, sporadic gifts
RELATIONSHIP STRENGTHS	Prioritizes equality in relationships, flexible but decisive, open to trying new things
RELATIONSHIP VULNERABILITIES	Lacks confidence, prone to feeling insecure in relationships or questioning partners' interest in them, small conflicts can feel like major threats
QUALITIES THEY VALUE MOST IN RELATIONSHIPS	Security, certainty, stability, loyalty, fun

Pitta-Kapha

OVERVIEW OF PITTA-KAPHA DOSHA		
ELEMENTS	Fire + Water + Earth	
ATTRIBUTES	· Warm · Heavy · Oily	· Liquid · Static · Slow
PHYSICAL TRAITS	· Average to large frame · Normal or combination skin · Pale or reddish skin · Medium to thick hair · Red or black hair	· Bigger teeth · Medium to large eyes · Blue or green eyes · Average to bulky muscle · Builds muscle easily
MENTAL CHARACTERISTICS	· Mental acuity and stamina · Focus	· Trustworthiness · Loyalty · Hospitality
COMMON IMBALANCES	· Hypertension · Congestive heart disease	· Skin conditions with exudate · Cancer

PITTA-KAPHA IN LOVE	
LOVE LANGUAGE	Love notes, touch, acts of kindness
RELATIONSHIP STRENGTHS	Good listener, makes partners feel seen, understanding, patient, committed, loyal
RELATIONSHIP VULNERABILITIES	Bears others' burdens, has trouble asking for help, doesn't state needs, internalizes problems, puts others' needs before their own
QUALITIES THEY VALUE MOST IN RELATIONSHIPS	Simplicity, depth, passion, time and space to pursue their own interests, loyalty

PITTA-KAPHA'S LIGHT AND SHADOW SIDES	
LIGHT	SHADOW
Stays steadily focused for long periods	Can become buried in work and have to forgo other opportunities
Cares for others and takes on extra responsibilities to help	Might lose touch with personal needs while overly focusing on others
Confident and certain of capabilities and skill sets	May have difficulty seeing that others aren't as capable or as sure of themselves
Has sustainable energy	Struggles with knowing when to stop or noticing when they are becoming sick

Vata-Kapha

OVERVIEW OF VATA-KAPHA DOSHA		
ELEMENTS	Ether + Air + Water + Earth	
ATTRIBUTES	Because the descriptors of ether, air, fire, water, and earth are opposites of one another, any combination of qualities can be seen in a vata-kapha person	
PHYSICAL TRAITS	Physical characteristics are quite variable due to the blend of contrasting elements. You may see extremes in this person, such as thin frame or tall frame, or they may have smaller eyes and thin lips but thick hair	
MENTAL CHARACTERISTICS	· Easygoing · Supportive	· Open-minded
COMMON IMBALANCES	· Unique sensitivities (generally higher sensitivities than other doshas and more deeply manifested conditions) · Respiratory conditions	· Allergies · Asthma · Swelling in joints · Poor circulation · Slow digestion

VATA-KAPHA'S LIGHT AND SHADOW SIDES	
LIGHT	SHADOW
Goes with the flow	Has trouble making decisions or asserting their own likes or needs
Prioritizes fun and ease	May avoid the hard work, especially when there isn't enough direction or there aren't big rewards
Likes to support others in achieving their goals	Might lack their own passion or area of focus for life
Friendly and strikes up conversation with anyone	Can have more talk than action, known to sit on the sidelines

VATA-KAPHA IN LOVE	
LOVE LANGUAGE	Words, touch, play
RELATIONSHIP STRENGTHS	Adaptable, supportive, joyful, fun
RELATIONSHIP VULNERABILITIES	Has the potential to lose their identity or merge with a partner's identity, avoids dealing with problems and conflict, sensitive, insecure
QUALITIES THEY VALUE MOST IN RELATIONSHIPS	Partner who wants to lead and make decisions, continued reassurance, reminders that they are valued

Tridosha

OVERVIEW OF TRIDOSHA	
ELEMENTS	Ether + Air + Fire + Water + Earth
ATTRIBUTES	Because tridosha means all elements are at play, it's difficult to state that any one descriptor prevails over another. Instead, we tend to find our tridoshic qualities in the middle of spectrums. For example, they are neither dry or oily, nor static or mobile— they are somewhere in between.
PHYSICAL TRAITS	In the tridoshic individual, we find physical characteristics to be very spread out among all the doshic traits. They can have any eye color or skin tone and an equal degree of all doshas means nothing will stand out as notably big or small.
MENTAL CHARACTERISTICS	Well-rounded, quick-thinking with mental stamina, good overall memory, may feel a range of emotions from anxiety to anger to sadness but without any one dominating, or without some of the interference emotion can cause
COMMON IMBALANCES	This dosha does not have common imbalances like the other doshas do. However, it is notable that if a tridoshic becomes imbalanced, their issues are more difficult to treat. The presence of all the doshas and elements means adjusting one can easily aggravate another.

Resources

In this book, we went in-depth on the emotional and mental aspects of the Ayurvedic doshas, but there's so much more to explore. The following resources can help you go deeper into some of the topics we merely touched upon:

Self-Care, Routine, and Lifestyle

The Ayurvedic Self-Care Handbook by Sarah Kucera
Living Ayurveda by Claire Ragozzino
Change Your Schedule, Change Your Life by Dr. Suhas Kshirsagar
The Path of Practice by Bri Maya Tiwari
Ayurveda Beginner's Guide by Susan Weis-Bohlen

Food and Herbs

What to Eat for How You Feel by Divya Alter
Root & Nourish by Abbey Rodriguez and Jennifer Kurdyla
The Yoga of Herbs by Dr. David Frawley and Dr. Vasant Lad
Ayurvedic Cooking for Beginners by Laura Plumb
Ayurvedic Medicine by Sebastian Pole
The Everyday Ayurveda Cookbook by Kate O'Donnell
The 3-Season Diet by John Douillard

Foundational/General

The Complete Book of Ayurvedic Home Remedies by Dr. Vasant Lad
Ayurveda: The Science of Self-Healing by Dr. Vasant Lad
Prakriti by Dr. Robert E. Svoboda
Ayurveda and the Mind by Dr. David Frawley

Acknowledgments

———

I'm humbled by the support I received while writing this book. Every word and act, no matter how large or small, was deeply meaningful to me. I'm especially grateful for:

Olivia Peluso, my editor, for sticking with me from start to finish, and all the chapter reorganizations in between. Thank you for your patience, experience, and time in shaping my ideas into something that can be shared with and beneficial to so many.

Hannah Matuszak, for your editing skills and assistance in fine-tuning this book in just the right spots and in all the right ways.

Jennifer Kurdyla, for your wisdom and heart. Your guidance and reassurance were exactly what I needed to keep going to see this book to fruition.

Steve Harris, my literary agent, for always being encouraging and helpful every step of the way.

My friends and family for always offering to lend a hand or a pep talk when my energy tank was low.

Douglas, for cheering me on, reminding me to take breaks, and making me dinner on long writing days. You're my favorite pitta-kapha.

All my teachers who have both trusted and empowered me with this knowledge, and the teachers that came before them. My hope is to always lead with the examples you have given me and to preserve the true essence and heart of Ayurveda.

About the Author

———

SARAH KUCERA, DC, CAP, is an Ayurvedic practitioner, chiropractor, and yoga teacher. She's the founder of Sage Center for Yoga & Healing Arts in Kansas City, Missouri, and the author of *The Ayurvedic Self-Care Handbook: Holistic Healing Rituals for Every Day and Season*. Kucera has a passion for teaching and empowering others to care for themselves with simple practices that can make a major impact on their health and in their lives.

sarahkucera.com | ⓘ **sarah_kucera**